Employee Engagement with Sustainable Business

Sustainability is a key issue for organisations: in the board room; with investors, customers and regulators; and with employees whose demands on organisations include improving their social and environmental performance in return for their loyalty and commitment. However, as well as being an important influence on why many organisations address their responsibilities and impacts, employees are also one of the most critical assets organisations can mobilise to manage their economic, social and environmental responsibilities successfully.

Research shows that various new types of employees are emerging and are vital in the pursuit of corporate sustainability. However, to date there is no one source that explores all of these types of employees and how they are involved in the sustainability process. This book fills that gap by highlighting five key types of employees, explaining recent research, providing case studies and giving analysis of the critical role of Social Intrapreneurs, Champions, Specialists, Godparents and Unsung Heroes. The book uses real-life examples with the latest research in an informative and accessible style. Management theory is used throughout – such as motivation, meaning of life, cultural mechanisms and organisational behaviour – but this is discussed through examples, rather than in a theoretical manner.

This book will provide insight, examples and practical advice on the different types of employees who do, or can, contribute to a sustainable world via the organisation they work for.

Nadine Exter is the Head of Business Development at the Doughty Centre for Corporate Responsibility, Cranfield University, UK. The author's proceeds from this book are being donated to the social movement making ecocide an international crime against peace: the law of ecocide.

Routledge Explorations in Environmental Studies

Employee Engagement with Sustainable Business

How to change the world whilst keeping your day job

Nadine Exter

Dear John,

Thank you so much for your kind words!

Nadine

Routledge
Taylor & Francis Group

LONDON AND NEW YORK

First published 2013
by Routledge
2 Park Square, Milton Park, Abingdon, Oxon OX14 4RN

Simultaneously published in the USA and Canada
by Routledge
711 Third Avenue, New York, NY 10017

Routledge is an imprint of the Taylor & Francis Group, an informa business

British Library Cataloguing in Publication Data
A catalogue record for this book is available from the British Library

Library of Congress Cataloging-in-Publication Data
Exter, Nadine.
   Employee engagement with sustainable business : how to change the
   world whilst keeping your day job / Nadine Exter.
       pages cm. – (Routledge explorations in environmental studies ; 5)
   Includes bibliographical references and index.
   1. Social responsibility of business. 2. Sustainable development.
   I. Title.
   HD60.E98 2013
   650.1–dc23   2012050802

ISBN: 978–0–415–53225–9 (hbk)
ISBN: 978–0–203–10984–7 (ebk)

Typeset in Sabon by
Swales & Willis Ltd, Exeter, Devon

Printed and bound by CPI Group (UK) Ltd, Croydon, CR0 4YY

'This book provides critical insight and best practices into how to inspire, equip and harness leaders and colleagues as passionate ambassadors and changemakers for the sustainable business of the future . . . both the theory and the practical cases enable the reader to consider the critical levers for building sustainability into the mindset and DNA of the organization.'
Lauren Iannarone, Head of Citizenship, Barclays Bank plc

'Employees: the missing link in too many company sustainability strategies, except when it comes to energy efficiency and recycling. But they can be the rocket fuel in successful corporate initiatives. Nadine Exter shows how.'
John Elkington, a world authority on corporate responsibility and sustainable development, Founding Partner & Executive Chairman of Volans, and author of most recent book Zeronauts

'Change is often instigated from above by a single charismatic leader. However, for the change to become permanent it is necessary for a mass of committed, innovative people to make it their own. This book is an overdue "tip of the hat" to all those who roll their sleeves up and make things happen.'
Paul Monaghan, Director, Up the Ethics, and former Head of Ethics and Sustainability at the Co-operative Group

'Finally, a book that can help us avoid the apocalypse described at its outset. Through the actions and social entrepreneurship – the difference making – of individuals in companies, the unsung heroes, sustainability specialists, social intrapreneurs, champions, and godparents, Nadine Exter offers us much needed hope that individual actions can make a huge difference in creating a world that all of our grandchildren can still live well in.'
Sandra Waddock, MA, MBA, DBA, Galligan Chair of Strategy and Professor of Management, Carroll School Scholar of Corporate Responsibility, Carroll School of Management, Boston College, USA

Contents

Illustrations

Acknowledgements

With thanks to all those interviewed and the many other change-makers out there, for your courage and for giving me hope. With thanks to the colleagues at the Doughty Centre for Corporate Responsibility, Cranfield University, for enabling this book to be written. Finally, with thanks to my family, for their constant support.

Abbreviations

AA	AccountAbility
ADP	Accenture Development Partnerships
ArupID	Arup International Development
BITC	Business in The Community
CBM	Consultative Business Movement
CR	corporate responsibility
CSR	corporate social responsibility
DOT	Do One Thing
FMCG	fast-moving consumer goods
GACSO	Global Association of Corporate Sustainability Officers
GDP	gross domestic product
GSK	GlaxoSmithKline
HR	Human Resources
IATA	International Air Transport Association
ISO	International Organization for Standardization
KPI	key performance indicator
CEO	Chief Executive Officer
CFO	Chief Financial Officer
GRI	Global Reporting Initiative
ISO	International Organization for Standardization
M&S	Marks & Spencer
MBA	Master of Business Administration
NBI	National Business Initiative
NED	non-executive director
NGO	non-governmental organisation
NFP	not-for-profit
PR	public relations
PRME	Principles of Responsible Management Education
R&D	research and development
ROI	return on investment
SAB	South African Breweries
SRI	socially responsible investment
UN	United Nations

UNHCR	United Nations High Commissioner for Refugees
USAID	United States Agency for International Development
VRIN	valuable, rare, inimitable and non-substitutable
VUCA	volatile, uncertain, complex and ambiguous

You too can make a difference
Imagine . . .[1]

It is 2040. You awake to a bright, cold, sunny morning, with dew in the air and the smell of smog gently wafting into the room; the traffic outside is only a low hum today. You can hear the sounds of your housemates as they go about their morning ablutions; the bathroom door creaks open and you jump out of bed and run to the bathroom before someone else gets there. Nowadays water is limited, of course, and if you are the last one to use the toilet it can get a bit smelly – the 'one flush per day per household' law has its smelly consequences! You wash with dry powder soap and shampoo, and clean your teeth with minty fresh waterless toothpaste tabs.

Your housemates are already at the breakfast table but you get priority seating, seeing as it's your house. Urban overcrowding and increased flooding in pretty much all coastal areas have pushed even more people into the cities, so when the government introduced the 'Vacant Room' law (if you have a vacant room in your house you have to rent it out), you welcomed strangers into your home.

Breakfast is a bowl of potato flakes in rice milk. Gone are the days of wheat and cow's milk for breakfast – bread, cereal, pancakes . . . plentiful in the memories of childhood! Oh, for a warm croissant, a knob of butter melting on top with a dollop of fresh raspberry jam. But when the global population exceeded nine billion ahead of schedule, land became even more at a premium. Farms, forests and green land had been converted into housing estates and shopping malls at an escalating rate since the turn of the century and, since we can't produce enough food for even half the population, rationing is commonplace. No more rampant capitalism!

There were warning signs – the food riots in Africa in the first decade of the twenty-first century continued into the second decade and eventually resulted in protectionism policies. In 2020 the multinationals that had bought swathes of land in Africa in order to export food to the developed countries were kicked out of the continent and the farming land was reclaimed for the Africans. However, it was not until the great famine of 2028 that realisation struck of how little food Western society could grow for all the hungry mouths. The price of food, clothing, heating and everyday staples was so high they just became unattainable. And even when these goods were available, the market by that point was controlled by a few large global companies that set prices so high, making billions of dollars in profits but paying no tax and rewarding shareholders with generous dividends to ignore their bad governance. The 2032 riots in New York, Paris, Cairo and Shanghai were especially vicious – thousands died when police and army opened fire on protesters and looters. Wall Street burned for three days and three nights. Things got better after the global stock-market system collapsed in 2033, forever changing the idea of money. The current system awards credits from work contributions which cannot be lent, borrowed, invested or exchanged except for food, housing and essentials. So it's potato flakes and rice milk for breakfast.

You wonder how your daughter is doing in China – she specialises in renewable electricity and works there. Although you miss her, you do know she is better off in China. As a member of the 'lost generation' – stuck between your generation that had comfortable, resource-wasteful childhoods and the current generation that blames you for the state of things – she is nevertheless one of the lucky ones. China invested heavily in renewable technologies after the turn of the century and as a consequence 'for all good jobs look East'. The quality of life is also better there – ironic given that China used to be the most polluting country on the planet.

You have a little habit before you set off for work: each day you calculate how many more years are left till retirement. Retirement age is now 76, so only 11.2 more years to go. Of course you know you are lucky; you have a stable job. Whilst the damage climate change inflicted on the natural world is raising the global temperature by at least three degrees – with all the anticipated consequences – it did mean a boom in the security, food production and 'green' technology industries. Funny that it used to be called 'green technology' as nowadays it's the only technology left, especially with oil so scarce. But it did mean that those with related specialities have secure jobs, and you happen to be one of those lucky people.

Another electricity shortage means the trains and buses are not operating again; it's been 15 years since you could afford to fuel or have a car, so you are walking to work today. You place the pollution protector mask over your face and head out on to the street.

The difference-makers

There is no doubt about the great global challenges we face in the decades to come; even climate change deniers admit that the supply of oil, water and natural resources is dwindling fast. The few rich have gotten richer whilst the many poor have gotten poorer; many areas where natural resources do exist are plagued by wars, conflict and ever-more aggressive competition for those scarce resources. Still too many people live in extreme poverty and others work in environments of prevalent racism, sexism and intergenerational inequality. The year 2040 is likely to be worse, and the scenario above could be considered a positive visioning of 2040; it is already the present-day experience of many millions of people. For them, this would be something to envy.[2]

But here's the great secret, the great hope – *it really doesn't have to be this way*! And not by giving up croissants and jam for breakfast, but by together taking small, simple actions that can have an immense effect. This is not a story of sadness, but one of hope, of courage and of action. Many may feel 'climate change fatigue' or 'environmental melancholia', or argue that the global consumerism system has to change first, and are not motivated enough or feel powerless to make a difference.[3] But there are still hundreds of thousands of people around the world getting involved to create a better future – taking control of their world and their actions, and making a difference. Some of them are profiled in this book: Priya, who works for Microsoft in the USA, calls it a 'grassroots movement'. Sumanta, who works for Olam in Indonesia, says it's simply the right way to think and act. Charlotte, working for Centrica in the UK, calls it her purpose, her way to help.

'Sustainability' as a term has now thankfully entered the lexicon of popular culture; it is recognised and oft used not just by specialists or politicians or in business but in civil society as well. Schools around the world run poetry competitions taking the theme of sustainability; documentary and feature films have been produced on the subject of sustainability – Ecotube (www.ecotube.com) and YouTube (www.youtube.com) feature some of these. There are some wonderful examples of public figures and popular movements advocating sustainability who have done much to further our understanding of why creating a sustainable world is so important. Well-known names include US politician Al Gore's education programme and documentary *An Inconvenient Truth*; UK actor Pete Postlethwaite campaigning for the environment and starring in *The Age of Stupid*; business woman Dame Anita Roddick setting up The Body Shop; and entrepreneur Ray Anderson advocating for industrial ecology and sustainability. They all have advanced the understanding of sustainability issues, helping to make 'sustainability' accepted and legitimate within our society.

And so as the concept of 'sustainability' has become more of a social norm, more and more individuals around the world are accepting responsibility for their actions and are taking on extra tasks at home and in their place of work. Many employees manipulate the corporate system,[4] change it or create new systems that enable positive action. Some of these individuals are profiled in this book and work in organisations that on the whole value employees and engage them in sustainability. The pay-back for these organisations is the emergence of engaged, responsible employees who create value for the organisation on multiple levels. New business opportunities, innovation, cost-saving, loyalty and new products and services are some of the organisational benefits realised. The benefit for individuals, in contrast, is inimitable: a job that aligns with their values and concerns, adds meaning to their life and becomes a job where they can take control of the impact they have on the world and truly make a unique difference.

The following chapters profile a selection of best-practice examples of individual employees around the world taking action to create societal or environmental good: the Unsung Heroes, the Specialists, the Social Intrapreneurs, the Champions and the Godparents. These types are somewhat interchangeable, but they are also unique in their specific role, impact and characteristics. Working in organisations that understand and take sustainability seriously, these employees are empowered into action because of their personal values and motivations, because of specific organisational enablers and because of wider societal change afoot. These employees work in a manner true to their personal values and bring individuality into a corporate system with great success, for themselves and for the corporations they work for.

Unsung Heroes

Often called the 'corporate system', organisations seem to develop a unique way of getting things done that almost develops a life of its own. People work within that system, sometimes developing it, encouraging it or trying to buck it. This 'way of getting things done' is in fact the organisational culture, and when strategically managed it can be positive for both organisational and individual success. However, not many organisations approach the system – the culture – as a strategic asset and as a consequence negative cultures and bad consequences can arise. 'Culture' is especially relevant for sustainability because being responsible – at both an individual and organisational level – is personal, complex and context-specific. In a few leading organisations there are individuals who recognise the importance of an engaged and positive culture and work strategically to develop and maintain this system. Once such company is a leading sustainable retailer in the UK called Marks & Spencer (M&S); a small team of individuals work within M&S to ensure the culture is positive and provides the foundations for success to flourish. These are the Unsung Heroes, quietly getting on with their jobs and passionate about creating a culture that enables and engages employees and contributes to the success M&S has achieved as a leading sustainable business.

Sustainability Specialists

An emerging profession, corporate Sustainability Specialists are employees whose job is to focus exclusively on helping their organisation become more sustainable. They are experts on a variety of related topics, and good generalists with solid business acumen. They could be part of a specific sustainability department, or an individual director working with Champions. As employees, Specialists are unique because they sit within the organisation and work to change the status quo, but also work very closely with external stakeholders as critical friends. The role is demanding – not only because it is still defining itself as a new profession and because we still do not have wholesale acceptance that sustainability is relevant to business – but also because of the unique skill set, knowledge and personal characteristics Specialists need to be good at their job. Profiled are six experienced specialists whose personal motivation, characteristics and effectiveness are helping to professionalise the specialism.

Social Intrapreneurs

Social Intrapreneurs are employees within an organisation who take direct action for innovations which address social or environmental challenges profitably. Social Intrapreneurs are a new type of employee that has emerged notably over the last decade. They take direct action by creating innovations that meet both social/environmental and corporate needs. They are determined, have a unique perspective of the role of business in society and also have a unique skill set, including entrepreneurial skills. Unlike social entrepreneurs working outside a for-profit business, Social Intrapreneurs believe that business can be a force for good whilst creating commercial value, and so work within organisations to create positive social change.

Champions

Champions are employees who support a cause or ideology and express this by taking on extra tasks and activities in their workplace. Their first profession is not sustainability, but they have a personal interest in an issue that is relevant to corporate sustainability, such as the environment, ethical trade or social cohesion. Champions support the efforts being made to create a sustainable organisation, helping to implement change within their own sphere of influence and in some instances initiating change across the organisation. They work with Sustainability Specialists and are effective because they are embedded within the organisation. They also have unique motivations and skills that enable them to become Champions. Profiled are a range of Champions from the very experienced to the determined new; Champions are not generation- or age-defined, but they do share a common mindset and skills.

Godparents

The idea of mentors is well known in business: (usually) middle or senior management employees who pass on support, guidance and advice to more junior members of staff. However, there is a type of employee who goes beyond mentoring; they help and advise the protégé to navigate the organisation as a political entity, and beyond this they take specific actions and interventions to enable their protégés in their work. Sustainability Godparents can be motivated by the desire to enable others, help junior members of staff develop or because they have a personal passion for sustainable business. Godparents are effective because they have legitimacy, contacts, influence and power. They do not need to be active change-makers themselves, but they help others to be effective through influencing, advising and enabling.

However – it is *not* enough that these extraordinary change-makers alone take action. Hope now lies not just with them, but with you as well. We can't outsource sustainability. In 2012 over three billion people around the world were employed – whether in for-profit, charity, private, social enterprises or public sector organisations (International Labour Office, 2012). Therefore, because it is us working in these businesses, we have significant power; we can make significant change. And businesses around the world understand this and are making commitments and advancing the knowledge and expertise of how to live sustainably (http://www.unglobalcompact.org/news/234-06-15-2012).[5]

Consider the commitments made by individual global citizens prior to the Rio 2012 Climate Change Summit: over *one billion* commitments were made to the Earth Day Network campaign A Billion Acts of Green (http://act.earth day.org). If you are one of the three billion employed, then it is likely that you, a family member, your neighbour or friend or colleague made a commitment to the campaign. As an employee you can get involved; you need to get involved.[6]

The following chapters profile five new types of employees who are emerging and taking action to create a more sustainable world. These are their stories, their actions. This is how they are changing the world without losing their day job. You may recognise yourself or friends and colleagues from their stories. These people are from all walks of life taking control and doing extraordinary things. But they are not actors, campaigners or politicians – they are your colleague sitting opposite you. They are the engineer building a bridge, the person supplying the coffee you drink. They are working from within organisations to make a difference. These are their stories. It could be yours.

> Sustainability is a grass-roots movement that can make a difference; it's about taking care of each other . . . it's a feeling that I could make a change. And we need to build a community of those interested . . . in being someone who wants to make the world better.
>
> (Priya, Microsoft – Sustainability Champion: see Chapter 4)

Introduction

Sustainability defined

The problem with sustainability is its very terminology. 'Sustainability' is an all-encompassing word, a much overused word. One that is so big a concept that it can become irrelevant to an individual, but also one so often used at a micro-level that it loses impact, such as on the packaging of a food item. People are passionate about sustainability – whether for or against. *But what does it mean?*

The clearest definition of sustainability derives from a United Nations commission convened in 1983 that interviewed hundreds of scientists, politicians, environmentalists and economists. In 1987 they released the report known as the Brundtland Report (United Nations, 1987; World Commission on Environment and Development, 1987). Chaired by Gro Harlem Brundtland, former Prime Minister of Norway, the Commission delivered the 'Brundtland definition of sustainable development'. 'Environment' is not just nature, but also where we live; and 'development' is what we do when we try to 'improve our lot'[1] within that environment – as individuals, companies or societies.

> Sustainable development is 'Development that meets the needs of the present without compromising the ability of future generations to meet their own needs'.
>
> (UN, 1987)

This definition is based on the understanding that, living on the same planet, we all have a common future: our lives are interlinked with those in different continents regardless of race, religion, generation, wealth, sex or status – and that what we do today will affect future generations (intergenerational justice). As such, we share the same limitations which are imposed by the state of technology and the limits of the environment to sustain life. The Commission further emphasised that priority should be given to the poorest, to help them meet their essential needs, such as food and water. Thus, although the concept of 'sustainability' has been around for centuries, the Brundtland Commission helped to articulate that being sustainable is about living within our limitations, respecting and managing better the impact we have both within our own species and interspecies, and intergenerational justice (i.e. what we do today cannot harm future generations).

Sustainability is not anticapitalism or antiprofit; sustainability advocates the right to meet our needs and to 'improve our lot' – but not at the expense of others (both born and generations to come). Since 1987 a plethora of ideas and related terminology has emerged: conscious capitalism, long-term capitalism, corporate social responsibility, corporate responsibility, corporate sustainability, shared value . . . For the purposes of this book, 'sustainability' is used in the context of the Brundtland definition. Being sustainable is predicated on the idea of being responsible (whether corporate, social or citizenship) and includes being responsible to the environment, our communities, our own workplace and in the marketplace as we strive to 'improve our lot' (Table 0.1).[2]

Table 0.1 The dimensions of sustainability: example impacts to consider

Environment	Pollution from our activities and the impact on climate change specifically (i.e. global warming)
	Pollution we produce (in water, air, soil/land, local environments) and the impact on species quality of life and ability to survive that pollution
	The waste we produce, both in utilising scarce resources and the subsequent pollution the waste causes
	Rare/scarce material resource overuse (plant and animal such as overfishing)
	Deforestation from our consumption and population growth activities
	Coastal erosion due to pollution and human activities
	Ecosystem degradation from human activities
	Impact of population growth on use of raw materials and resources
	Dwindling stocks of green, forest and agricultural land from human land use
	Surface and regeneration damage from human use (dredging, mining, etc.)
	Food security because of growing population, overuse of natural resources and our own activities impact on our ability to produce food (i.e. pollution, land use for non-food-producing reasons)
	Fresh water shortages because of land misuse, pollution and climate change
	Flooding because of land misuse, pollution and climate change
	Threats to biodiversity and species survival from human activity
	Ocean acidification from pollution
	Energy and fuel depletion because natural resources are being overused or polluted
Community	Community wellbeing: how business interacts and impacts communities, such as community investment and being a fair neighbour
	Economic renewal: the economic and social wellbeing of communities' business impact and need for their own survival (i.e. health, social housing)
	Education: supporting the education of young and local people as future employees, suppliers, politicians, etc.

Table 0.1 Continued

	Employability: helping to build the skills needed for the workplace of today and tomorrow Volunteering: employees volunteering their time or part of their salaries to community causes they are passionate about Demographics: urbanisation as people move into cities for work; how business fairly responds to demographic changes such as population growth, ageing population, the growing middle class, gender trends, migration, ethnic shifts. Corporate discrimination based on age, gender, religion or colour
Marketplace	Impact of lobbying and political contributions (responsible lobbying) Impact of how organisations are competitive and competitors in the marketplace Supply chain management and practices' impact on suppliers, competitors and other market members Impacts of organisational product and service innovation (responsible innovation) How customers are treated and impact of marketing activities (responsible marketing, accurate product labelling etc.) Impact from products: product responsibility The use of child and forced labour in the supply chain The use of investment in responsible ways The effect of protectionism and regional policies from corporate influence The impact bribes/facilitation payments have in the longer term Stakeholder access to information: fair access to information with transparency and disclosure Impact on economies' in the supply chain ability to thrive Tax paying as corporate citizens to be responsible and proportionate to the impact created in pursuit of growth/sales Accounting and reporting as responsible and a positive contribution to society
Workplace	The impact of employee representation: to be fair and equal Treatment of disabilities and minorities in a responsible and fair manner The impact of diversity, inclusion and equality (and discrimination of all forms) to create a fairer and more equal society Working practices that are fair Health and wellbeing of employees Reward and remuneration in a responsible way Impact of how organisations respect human and labour rights The impact on own operations and stakeholders from governance standards

Compiled from: US National Intelligence Council (2012). *Global Trends* 2030; *BITC Classification*. Online at: www.bitc.org.uk/issues; KPMG (2012). *Expect the Unexpected: Building Business Value in a Changing World*. Online at: www.kpmg.com/Global/en/Issues AndInsights/ArticlesPublications/Pages/building-business-value.aspx; Ashridge (2005). Catalogue of CSR activities: a broad overview. Produced for the Danish Commerce and Companies Agency; and Rockström J, Steffen W, Noone K, Persson A, Chapin FS, Lambin E, Lenton TM *et al.* (2009). Planetary boundaries: exploring the safe operating space for humanity. *Ecology and Society* 14 (2): 32.

Thus, sustainability is not only about the environment and climate change, eco-efficiency, water shortages, pollution or food shortages. It is also about how we treat our neighbours, our employees, our suppliers. It is also about how we act as citizens, such as paying fair tax, competing fairly and adhering to the laws and ethical norms of our societies. It is about long-term, inclusive and responsible thinking and action.

Theories explained

Sustainability is a relatively new field of management study in academia, related to the rise of the modern environmentalism/ecology social movement. It has risen in importance so recently in part because it is only in the last 30 years that our scientific understanding of and the science behind sustainability have really become established.[3] But by its very definition, 'sustainability' relates to every aspect of a business – it is truly cross-functional. Although sustainability as a specialism is undoubtedly growing and emerging, there is an almost universal agreement among those of us working in the field that (although sustainability experts are needed to inform, guide and advise) sustainability relates to each component part of a business and the business as a whole. Thus, we look to other disciplines within management and environmental sciences for ideas, advice and theories. As physicist Albert Einstein said: we can't solve problems by using the same kind of thinking we used when we created them. Somewhat unusually for academia, we have to work embedded within the business world and interpret theories from different disciplines for answers: within management theory for change management, organisational behaviour, people management, to leadership, but also within environmental sciences, psychology and sociology.

This book profiles five employee types that have emerged within the sustainability movement. Through a series of desk research, interviews and then data analysis I interpreted and identified what they were doing and why.

1. What emerged was a sense that they were part of a larger movement – a global social movement.
2. To understand why specific employees take action, I developed a five-stage individual development framework and from this various theories became relevant: meaning of life, a sense of self (ego, identity theory and collectivism theory), the development of values and characteristics (learned experiences), motivation and commitment, and dissonance reduction/conflict resolution.
3. When exploring how specific employees were successful the following management disciplines were helpful and included in advice given within the following chapters: change management theory; the skills of communication and engagement; and the role of critical organisational enablers such as organisational culture, job discretion, the role of leaders and corporate agendas.

Whereas this book does not profile management theory as a stand-alone discipline, relevant theories are interpreted for the context of this research, and briefly introduced and discussed in the context of each chapter. What follows now is a more detailed description of the main theories used throughout the book.

Global social movement theory

A social movement is a group of people with a common ideology trying together to achieve certain goals. They are usually informal groupings and sometimes individual members may not be aware of the wider social movement occurring. Social movements have occurred throughout history and are seen as how transformation occurs from one form of society to another – for example, from pre- to post-industrial, the abolition of the slave trade when it became socially abhorrent, urbanisation over the last 200 years, and the opposition of Western colonisation in the nineteenth century. Thought to be enabled by the spread of democracy over the last 200 years, social movements can be expressions of dissidence or wide-scale social change (Snow *et al.,* 2004; Hawken, 2008).

The term 'new social movements' refers to a large collection of new movements that have arisen in the last 50 years, especially in post-industrial economies (Pichardo, 1997). New social movements focus not on material goals but on social goals such as human rights. This makes them very different to previous social movements. Examples include the antiapartheid movement, the labour movement, the women's movement and the gay rights movement. New social movements are informally and loosely organised and can be global in scale. It is commonly accepted that a 'new social movement' includes the ecology movement (environmentalism[4]) and the corporate responsibility movement (Bendell, 2009).

> A key shift that was consolidated . . . is the change in the way many business people relate to the social and environmental performance of their companies.
>
> (Bendell, 2009)

Corporate sustainability refers not just to ecological issues but also to social and economic issues. The academic Jem Bendell argues that a new social movement has been occurring in the business world, which I concur with and observed further during the research for this book. This new social movement can be seen as an inevitability when considering: the growing power – and therefore more obvious impact – of corporations in the capitalist systems across the world; a shift of those who would have been campaigners in the 1960s moving into for-profit organisations to work; the professionalisation of campaigning groups such as World Wildlife Fund and the Fairtrade organisation; the growing awareness in the general public (i.e. as customers and employees) of global issues through the internet and global media channels; the increased data now available on global trends, poverty and economic inequality, human rights violations, climate change, oil reserves and ecological damage from oil exploration and how this affects resource and business operations; or the politicisation of such issues and pan-global political organisations' attempts to address them (such as the United Nations establishing a committee on the human environment in 1972) – or a combination of all of the above.

What is clear is that social movements are placing continued pressure on corporations and governments across a variety of sustainability-related issues, such as most recently the global Occupy movement (Flank, 2011), the Uncut and Tax Justice Network movements (www.taxjustice.net/cms/front_content. php?idcatart=2&lang=1) and An Economy for the 99% movement (www. wdm.org.uk/event/economy-99-programme).

Why employees take action

A literature search and review at the start of any research project help to frame relevant theories and the questions that will be asked when interviewing subjects for case studies. What emerged from my interpretation of the literature review for this book – reinforced and shaped by the empirical research – is a five-stage developmental framework from the viewpoint of an individual. The model helps to show the journey and influences individuals undergo which results in them becoming employees who will take action for sustainability. Such a model is not uncommon in academia; taking a viewpoint from the individual's perspective rather than from outside the individual helps to capture a variety of influences on, and the complexities of, the human psyche (Collier and Esteban, 2007; Parker *et al.*, 2010). What we[5] found is that it is not only influences and values of adult life that create corporate sustainability change-makers; rather the change-makers' developmental journey starts in their childhood. The detailed case studies included in the following chapters reflect this journey, clearly showing the influence early learned experiences had on them in becoming the change-makers they are today. Table 0.2 shows these developmental stages.

What is unusual about this model is that it interprets theories across sociology and management.

Meaning of life, sense of self and the emergence of a change champion

To answer the question of why someone wants to be a change-maker, I looked to and connected relevant theories and observations, such as from notable neurologist Sigmund Freud. Freud defined three parts of the human psyche: id, ego and super-ego. Id is the unconscious part of ourselves that incorporates our basic instinctive drives (e.g. for food and shelter, fight or flight, reproduction). Super-ego includes our ideals, spiritual goals and our

Table 0.2 Hypothesised sustainability change-maker developmental stages

Development stage	Description	Observations
Early/young adult personal development	Early influences that helped to shape an individual's *values*, whether influences or experiences. These help develop fixed values, and create a *seed* and often an *awakening* moment for future possible action. With the change-makers, these early *learned experiences* influenced initial career choices and personal *characteristics* of how (*skills*) and why (*motivation*) they do their job; these learned experiences had an impact on their desires to find meaning from the workplace as a significant contribution to developing *meaning of self*, and *meaning of their lives*	All employee types discussed in the book developed in their childhood an awareness of larger political, societal or environmental concerns; most were exposed to these through international experiences, familial influence or by where they were brought up (countryside versus city). These seemed to place a 'seed' in their sense of self of interest in sustainability that could later be awakened. All seem to have high levels of fixed values that give them confidence to take action. Social Intrapreneurs and Specialists seem to have higher levels of interest in sustainability-related issues tied to their understanding of the meaning of their lives. Champions and Godparents seem to take satisfaction in being change-makers and having a unique identity in the organisation, perhaps more so than Specialists and Social Intrapreneurs, who seem more driven to create social and environmental value
Relationship with organisation	What influenced the *attraction* to work for their employer and what keeps them *motivated* to work there and *committed* to the organisation. Unconscious *signals* from the corporate agenda to tone from the top and reputation. The degree of either *values congruence* or the personal ability to *make a difference*. *Social identity* of the organisation as a collective and how this feeds into *personal identity*. The learned experiences in the workplace. Experiences that created an 'awakening' of the 'seed' planted in their childhood to have an interest in sustainability	Overall, all the employee types have strong connections to their organisations, albeit for different reasons. All use their workplace as a source of meaning of their lives, as a way to reinforce their self-identity (sense of self) and an avenue to express or reinforce their values. All have similar views of the role and responsibility of business, although Specialists and Social Intrapreneurs seem to be more determined that their organisations enhance that role. Many of the employees experienced an awakening moment during a work experience, whether current or past employment

Table 0.2 Continued

Development stage	Description	Observations
Disconnect/trigger event that leads to conflict or opportunity	This relates to a more specific time and place where the individual experiences either a positive or negative event. This could be an opportunity such as a new job, or an experience such as witnessing negative action on the part of employer, colleagues or in the wider world. This could create a disconnect of expected corporate action or values and the individual attempts to reduce this disconnect (*dissonance reduction*), unsatisfactory levels of *self-control* and self-destiny creation, or changed perspectives of the organisation and thus harming work being a source of meaning for them (*psychological contract* with the organisation damaged). Often positive triggers occur, such as identifying a business service or product, being given an opportunity by the employer or creating an opportunity by interpreting the corporate agenda and building a business case	The empirical research phase showed that in fact there was not commonly a specific time or place where disconnect or opportunity occurred. Rather, a series of smaller events led to an opportunity such as a job, or disconnect such as the identity clash and related relationship the individual had with the organisation needing to be addressed (and the individual takes action to rectify that relationship). With Champions often an opportunity was given because the individual was well respected and efficient, and only after being able to align personal interest in sustainability with the new tasks does the champion then flourish as a sustainability change-maker
The individual's initial response	The first reaction that the individual had – most notably, *'fight or flight'*. This first reaction is dependent on individual characteristics as well as *organisational enablers*, such as providing fair opportunities for employees, and a listening and learning culture	The initial response was shown to be critical to the path the change-maker then took. Opportunities that were presented were taken for a variety of personal reasons, but those initial opportunities were significant in allowing the journey to continue to the point of individuals becoming successful change-makers. Individual characteristics helped to shape how they responded, such as having fixed values they would not compromise, as well as organisational enablers such as an engaged culture and sustainability

being seen as a legitimate business issue. Events that led to disconnect could result in either the person leaving to find opportunities elsewhere (and Social Intrapreneurs and Specialists will more readily do this), become frustrated change-makers (as Champions can be), or stay and create or seize the opportunities

Successful action did seem to cascade into further successful action, and reinforce employees' relationships with the organisation and their desires to continue as sustainability change-makers. Some specific critical success factors were observed:

- Discretion/space in their job role to take on action, explore, experiment and take action outside their expected job description
- Access to information, networks and relevant sustainability experts (inside or outside the organisation). As most were intellectually curious, this also helped to satisfy a learning need
- The tone set by the organisation, mainly by leaders and direct line managers. Whether the espoused values of the organisation, levels of engagement or the signals sent of what was on the corporate agenda and was permissible to address
- Power of one sort or another. Four types were identified which varied significantly in use across the employee types: borrowed, earned authority, positional power, entrepreneurial power
- Personal skills of communicating, ideas generation, negotiating, building allies, selling and determination/drive

Action and outcome

The action the individual then takes and the corresponding success/failure is influenced by a variety of factors: if the person is *motivated* enough to move from *passive* to *non-passive action*, if the person cares enough about the issue and the organisation; and if there are *organisational enablers* in place such as *discretion* to be successful in tasks, leaders who understand and support the individual and the *culture* of the organisation conscience. Ego is about how we define our reality and our sense of self ('a set of psychic functions such as judgment, tolerance, reality testing, control, planning, defence, synthesis of information, intellectual functioning, and memory'). Ego contributed to understanding the motivations of change-makers because ego specifically helps us to organise our thoughts and make sense of them and the world around us (Freud and Bonaparte, 2009). But not everyone organises their thoughts with the same success; we develop different degrees of clarity and sense of who we are as individuals and in the world around us. In simplistic terms, we have variations of success on the clarity we have of our values, our characteristics and cognitive reasoning; and variations of success in understanding the 'place' or unique identity we have in the world – the 'meaning of our lives'.

Academics Reker and Wong (1988; Reker *et al.*, 1987) define meaning of life as:

> The cognisance of order, coherence, and purpose in one's existence, the pursuit and attainment of worthwhile goals, and an accompanying sense of fulfilment.

Therefore, we look for sources that will provide clarity as to the meaning of our lives. Scientist Viktor Frankl identified four sources of meaning: through spiritual aspirations, through our deeds (i.e. work), through our experience of values (which can also be in the workplace) and through our attitudes. He further postulated that finding these sources of meaning (such as a job providing opportunities for deeds and experiences of values) can reinforce one's sense of self (Frankl, 1964; Visser, 2008).

In management theory this 'search for meaning' relates to the relationship we seeks with our place of work. This is because our self-classification (how we try to define our sense of self) tends to be in a social context: from the categories of social groupings[6] we are members of, such as family, religion, nation and workplace (Evans and Davis, 2001). We look for, prescribe to or seek to reinforce our self-identity from those memberships by seeking out similarities in values, characteristics, meaning or opportunity. If there is congruence of values (which is important because of what Frankl noted about the meaning we can derive from our experiences of values), specifically between ourself and our work grouping, then we can create work as being a source of meaning. This can also result in positive employee attitudes, job satisfaction and commitment (Amos and Weathington, 2008; Turker, 2009).

However, as well as our attraction to groupings we sometimes look for distinctiveness or uniqueness, sometimes from aspirational or inspirational sources. This further helps to define our distinctiveness and expression of self (ego) (Amos and Weathington, 2008). So we can have two dimensions working at the same time (and sometimes conflicting with each other) in our subconscious efforts to define our sense of self and the meaning of our life: from social groupings such as at work, and as a unique individual.

Positively for organisations, creating or reinforcing our identity (social and individual) can positively impact on our individual organisational citizenship behaviours. But if something occurs that disrupts that identity, then the resulting impact may not just affect our *behaviour*; it can cascade into affecting our sense of self (our *ego*) as well – because the two so often are connected (Whitehouse, 2006). A negative disruption can lead to conflict and, if concern is high enough about that conflict, then we will move from being passive champions to active ones (Bansal, 2003). Thus the employee change-agent is born.

Organisational culture and engaging and motivating employees to be responsible

'Organisational culture' is the phrase used when referring to the collective behaviour of individuals in an organisation: a set of shared assumptions that guide interpretation (and motivation) and action (Ravasi and Schultz, 2006). Sometimes called 'the corporate system', it is 'the way things get done around here' (Deal and Kennedy, 1982; Drennan, 1992). A bad organisational culture can discourage talent from joining and disrupt the effectiveness of an organisation; conversely, a good culture can attract and retain great talent over and above competitors.[7] Organisational culture is not an abstract idea; rather it is an intangible asset that is responsible for 'the way things get done' in an organisation – a continuous, reinforcing cycle of motivation to behave in a certain way when carrying out workplace duties.

For example, an employee may be driven by a personal motivation to carry out a specific behaviour for the organisation – such as securing recycled materials for an organisation's products – because it reinforces the employee's individual and work identity of caring for the environment or that person's contribution to the organisation. This creates an outcome at the individual level; however this also has a positive outcome at the organisational level through security of supply and retaining talent. There can also be negative examples though – for example, when an individual is motivated by personal reward to undertake a behaviour that could be immoral or illegal. We have seen motivation and behaviours working to create negative outcomes in the financial sector: when personal reward (motivation) is not representative of the effort to achieve, or the impact of, the outcome, then this reward can lead to a negative set of behaviours that becomes 'normal' inside the organisation (although often not normal outside the organisation). And that normality further motivates the employee to continue acting in a negative way, even if it is something that person would not think of doing in other social groupings. Thus, this motivation plus behaviour becomes part of the culture of the organisation.[8]

Culture can be diagnosed and managed, and an engaged culture can significantly enable an organisation to be sustainable as it encourages employees to reinforce their personal values through positive citizenship behaviour.

Thus, planned actions can create a culture where positive citizenship behaviour is the norm, such as:

- Utilising tone from the top (the message and signals that organisational leaders send – helping to create motivation)
- Cleverly using organisational agendas (what the organisational leaders tells stakeholders they think is and is not relevant to address, and if that knowledge cascades through the ranks accurately and fairly – also affecting motivation)
- Developing a specific organisational identity or brand that the individual wants to identify with (affecting motivation)
- And developing policies and procedures that encourage positive behaviour and specific employee intervention policies (such as giving an employee job discretion to experiment, using total reward packages that measure longer-term and holistic outcomes, and 360-degree feedback (Exter, 2011)).

This is explored specifically in Chapter 1.

Methodology

The purpose of this book is to understand what is occurring in the real world now within the employee base in relation to contributions towards creating sustainable organisations and environments; to understand and postulate why; and then share these stories with practical advice on how any employee can get involved. Therefore it was important to capture existing practice – an action research approach – but to be guided in the initial research by management theory and then subsequently ground observations in those theories found relevant. This book is part of an ongoing research project, and previous research had identified the types of employees emerging (Unsung Heroes, Specialists, Social Intrapreneurs, Champions and Godparents) as well as what leading sustainable organisations were doing to engage employees en masse with responsible and sustainable business. A sixth type was also identified: Leaders of organisations, whether at the very top of the organisational hierarchy (i.e. Chief Executive Officer (CEO), Chief Financial Officer (CFO), non-executive directors – (NEDs)) or senior management. However, much has been researched and written on organisational leadership for sustainability, whereas relatively little has been written on what is occurring within the ranks of organisations. It was therefore decided not to focus on organisational leaders; please see Further Reading for suggestions of good books on leadership for sustainability.

Two main data sources were used:

1. A literature search across both academic and practitioner literature, including case studies, business reports and, for the Specialist chapter

(Chapter 2), job boards and job descriptions, and, for the Champions chapter (Chapter 4), corporate websites and sustainability reports. A set of key search terms were developed (level 1 and 2 field key words) and literature sources identified, tested and reviewed, expanded and then refined. The resulting analysis was refined and themes were clustered.

2. Empirical data was collated in the form of a series of interviews with each of the employee types described in the book. Research was first done to identify potential interviewees. It was decided to use best-practice examples in order to produce advice, but otherwise no restrictions were placed on inclusion criteria – a spread of highly experienced to emerging best practice was used, across age, gender and region. Ability to identify, contact and gain access was a limitation. Not all interviewees are included in the book, as many asked to remain anonymous, but their data was included in the conversation analysis and subsequent observations shared. Conversation analysis was done for each interview, and then again across the interviews for each employee type to observe similarities and differences. Finally, an analysis was done across all those interviewed to highlight recurring themes, such as social movement theory, meaning of life and motivation.

The initial literature review was then refined to an estimated 60 peer-reviewed academic papers (numerous practitioner-based reports and information are also used and referenced) and a set of specific theories were identified as relevant to the observations from the empirical data. These are detailed in 'Theories Explained', above. Finally the results were reviewed by colleagues and those interviewed, and the book written.

The opinions and views expressed in the personal stories are not those of the author or Cranfield University. Effort has been made to do due diligence when choosing the case studies, and as far as it is possible to confirm, the author believes that those interviewed and profiled were honest and shared personal experiences and insight. The author gives thanks to those interviewed for that privilege.

Further reading

Leadership for sustainability

AccountAbility Institute (2012). *Insights from Corporate Leaders*. London: AccountAbility.

D'Amato A, Henderson S, Florence S (2009). *CSR and Sustainable Business: A Guide to Leadership Tasks and Functions*. Greensboro, NC: CCL Press. Online at: www.ccl.org/leadership/pdf/research/CorporateSocialResponsibility.pdf.

Elkington J (2012). *The Zeronauts*. Abingdon, Oxon: Routledge.

Gitsham M, Lenssen G, Quinn L, de Bettignies HC, Gomez J, Oliver-Evans C, Zhexembayeva N, *et al*. *Developing the Global Leader of Tomorrow*. Ashridge: UK. www.unprme.org/resource-docs/DevelopingTheGlobalLeaderOfTomorrow Report.pdf.

Ladkin D (2010). *Rethinking Leadership*. Cheltenham: Edward Elgar.
Marshall J, Coleman G, Reason P (2011). *Leadership for Sustainability*. Sheffield: Greenleaf.

Key concepts

Carson R (1962). *The Silent Spring*. Boston, MA: Houghton Mifflin: USA.
Collier J, Esteban R (2007). Corporate social responsibility and employee commitment. *Business Ethics: A European Review* 16 (1): 19–33.
Fuchs C (2006). The self-organisation of social movements. *System Practice and Action Research* 19 (1): 101–137.
Leopold A (1949). *A Sand County Almanac*. New York: Oxford University Press.
Lovelock J (1979). *Gaia: A New Look at Life on Earth*. Oxford: Oxford University Press.
Parker SK, Bindl UK, Strauss K (2010). Making things happen: a model of proactive motivation. *Journal of Management* 36 (4): 827–856.
Reker GT, Wong PTP (1988). Aging as an individual process: Toward a theory of personal meaning. In JE Birren & VL Bengston (Eds.) *Emergent Theories of Aging* (pp. 214–246). New York, NY: Springer.
Reker GT, Peacock EJ, Wong PT (1987). Meaning and purpose in life and well-being: A life span perspective. *Journal of Gerontology* 42: 44–49.
Visser W (2008). *Making a Difference: Purpose-Inspired Leadership for Corporate Sustainability and Responsibility (CSR)*. Saarbrücken: VDM.

1   Unsung Heroes

Unsung Heroes: Individuals within an organisation quietly working to create a responsible and engaged organisational culture that enables sustainable business to flourish. They are called Unsung Heroes because the work they do is not always obvious – they create an engaged and responsible culture that becomes 'the way things get done around here', rather than a celebrated project or business win.

In 2007 leading UK retailer Marks & Spencer (M&S) set out a bold vision: to create an organisation that would be a leading example of a responsible and sustainable retailer – to be the greenest (now termed 'sustainable') retailer in the UK by 2012. It was bold because at the time they committed themselves to investing an estimated £40 million per annum for five years towards achieving this goal and were unsure if this investment would be repaid; because they committed themselves to doing this whilst competitively growing and succeeding economically. It was bold because at that time only a handful of for-profit businesses believed being sustainable also made good economic sense and had committed wholly to becoming a sustainable business; because at that time there was still not enough data to prove being sustainable was financially rewarding; and because few business models existed to help a business undertake this sort of change process.

Sir Stuart Rose, the Chief Executive Officer (CEO) at the time, gave his organisation five years to achieve a 100-point plan (80 more targets were added in 2010). Called Plan A – because there is no Plan B for the one planet we have – the plan included ambitious targets such as turning M&S carbon-neutral by 2012 and impacting over three billion individual items that M&S purchases, manufactures and sells. Plan A involved changing how M&S operates in every way. But Sir Stuart Rose and his team had faith in M&S:

> If an organisation with 70,000 people decides it wants to do something, I promise you, this is the organisation to do it.
>
> (Sir Stuart Rose, 2007)

From 2007 to 2012 Plan A delivered a financial net benefit to M&S of £185 million (including £105 million in 2011–12 alone). In 2012 M&S became carbon-neutral, sent zero waste to landfill and reduced packaging use by 26%. Numerous awards and recognition have helped M&S as a brand and with gaining strong customer loyalty. Other organisations now look to M&S for advice on how they can undertake the sustainability journey. In 2010–11 the new CEO, Marc Bolland, continued the commitment of Plan A and announced the follow-up ambition of M&S: to be the world's leading sustainable major retailer by 2015.

The success of the past five years would not have been achievable if M&S as a whole had not supported and engaged with Plan A. A significant contribution to the company's success is because every employee was encouraged to get involved; Plan A became part of the language, goals and targets, and purpose of the business. In essence Plan A became a significant influence on the culture of the organisation and that organisational culture was strategically planned and managed, with specific experts working on the culture and engaging all employees so that Plan A could work. In turn, Plan A has become a key driver of employee engagement and recruitment and retention.

This chapter explores the strategic approach M&S took to engage employees in sustainability. It uncovers some critical Unsung Heroes working behind the scenes to create a culture of engagement that enabled success. The success of M&S is unique; but there are lessons to be learned that other organisations can utilise to help them on their own sustainability journey.

1.1 Case studies

Sarah Findlater, Head of Employee Engagement, M&S (UK and International)

We think M&S is special, because of our strong roots and heritage but also because we continue to evolve and innovate and so we are excited about and ambitious for our future. We are proud that we do business ethically and responsibly and we care about the world, our customers and colleagues and the communities we work amongst. As a result we inspire great trust and pride and passion and all those things are incredibly important to us.

The business is very invested in employees being engaged. But framing this mindset was not an overnight achievement. We have been running an engagement survey for five years and have worked hard to demonstrate the commercial value that highly engaged teams bring to the business in real terms. Nailing the evidence through robust data correlation has enabled our senior leadership teams to see the link between employee engagement scores and performance. Now the case is proven they are pushing for more information, and engagement is a much higher priority.

However, I would say it was probably in 2010 when we really got very strategic with how we create a culture of engagement and recognised the need for a more sophisticated approach. That is when the Centre of Expertise for Engagement was formed, a dedicated central team in Human Resources (HR) that focuses on creating an engaged culture and workforce and tasked with the development of the engagement strategy. As part of this, the engagement team took responsibility for the People part of Plan A commitments [previously responsibility of the Plan A team]; Plan A is really key in helping us to attract talent, engage employees, and helping us create pride and therefore it forms an important part of our employer brand. It gives us lots of engagement opportunities both in terms of increasing passion for the business but also in terms of enabling our people to play their part in Plan A. Engagement is now a business KPI [key performance indicator] for each manager – something the commercial teams asked for.

Of course, as with any organisation, we have 'our way' of doing things, our unique culture. We can be quite traditional in our processes and so change can sometimes be hard for people. We want our people to join in and contribute and so we work to provide opportunities for people to share their views. We invest a lot of time in explaining 'the why' to people; we want our colleagues to understand what we stand for, where we are going and how they fit into that.

As a big company there is also a risk of silos forming. This can be a positive thing because it helps to create close-knit teams and loyalty, but it can also get in the way when different parts of the business work together. We have recently launched an organising principle to galvanise the business to work really collaboratively for the benefit of the customer. It is called 'In Touch' and it is all about developing a mindset that encourages us to be more in touch with each other, with our customers and with the outside world. We launched about five initiatives to help get things going, such as sharing information on what different teams across the business are achieving, and encouraging colleagues to go out to stores and other departments for two to five days a year to really see what they are up to. The point is that they come back with a broader perspective and use their new insights to inform their decision making and business planning.

It is important to have a culture where every employee has a voice and an avenue to express that voice and can contribute to the business. We need actual mechanics to allow this. So we have a formal employee representative group, a Directors' breakfast once a month to gather feedback and views, we have a 'Big' idea scheme to encourage ideas to specific business challenges, and we educate our leaders on the importance of authentic listening. We have a dedicated section on the intranet with tools to help managers engage their team and create the conditions for a strong engagement culture, tips and advice across a range of subjects, we share success stories, and for those interested we give background information on specific aspects of engagement. This culture of engagement is a business priority for us.

Sarah joined M&S on the HR Graduate Scheme and has worked in various generalist and specialist HR roles throughout her 13 years there. Sarah was promoted to Head of Employee Engagement in 2011, where she has overall responsibility for Employer Brand and Employee Engagement Strategy, our People Plan A proposition, Employee Health and Wellbeing and the People Policy Specialist function. She is also a member of the M&S HR Leadership Team.

Sophie Brooks, Employee Engagement, M&S (UK)

I have the best job in the world! I sit between the Plan A team and the HR Engagement team and focus on the 'People' part of Plan A. I look at external people-focused drivers that can help create an engaged workforce and help us to be a responsible business delivering on our objectives and commitments. So I focus on five areas: employability, volunteering as an engagement tool, local fundraising to encourage community, diversity and wellbeing. As an umbrella to these areas I work on local community involvement.

My role was originally about charity partnerships, but Plan A is not about charity and it became clear that the role needed to be more strategic. The five areas were identified as existing but not strategic engagement tools, which they are, so they were pulled together in 2010 for one person to lead and my role moved to the Engagement team. All five areas are commitments we have made in Plan A, but more than that, they are also about creating an engaged culture and motivating the workforce. The two are integral.

'Employability' is a big area I work on. We get a huge return here on engagement levels because it provides motivation for how individual employees can contribute, provides a sense of community and corporate identity, and helps our employees really see the impact of their good actions – generating a pride to work for M&S. Essentially, 'employability' is about creating jobs and helping people overcome barriers to work.

Marks & Start is our flagship employability programme which started back in 2004 when we asked our customers and employees who they wanted to see us support into work. The groups they chose were single parents, those with disabilities, young people and those at risk of homelessness. We work with four charity partners [Gingerbread, Remploy, the Prince's Trust and Business in The Community (BITC)] to deliver this programme, providing pre-employability training, a two-week placement in M&S and post-placement support. When the individual is on the placement in our stores or offices we assign a buddy to them and engage the immediate employee team to help. The 'buddy' is a role any employee can take on if they want to do a little bit more in their day job; it helps train our staff and show employees up close the impact of what we do. About 80% of those placed become accredited, which means if a job arises in M&S they don't have to go for interview, or even apply online, they can simply go straight into the role – that is the real beauty of the programme. Critically, 98% of those in the programme (those placed) say it is a positive experience and 40–50% who go through the M&S programme are employed after three months of their placement.

There are some areas that still need work however. We have historically had a leading diversity offer, but we know we need to move this on and be strategic about embedding the business case in order to continue to be an employer of choice for women, those from ethnic minorities and those of all ages.

For all our programmes there are soft and hard impacts, which is important to track and show how the programme is affecting engagement and therefore loyalty, performance and productivity. We are exploring an Employee Happiness Index and a Social Return on Investment indicator because we greatly invest in our programmes and so it is necessary to show the return. But if we had not taken that leap of faith in the beginning then we would not be where we are now. To prove these schemes are working – and that essentially my role is worth investing in – we monitor our engagement scores, which are good. We get a 90% response rate on the staff survey and from that about 75% score of employees feeling engaged [assessed via a series of specific engagement questions]. If something makes sense to us, we will experiment and try it a bit, see the 'soft' impacts. If we can prove the business case from that, then it expands. That is very much the way we do things here.

Sophie joined M&S in commercial management in a retail context, where she saw firsthand the benefits of developing and inspiring a committed and engaged workforce to deliver key priorities. In March 2012 Sophie joined the Employee Engagement team where she manages People Plan A.

Mike Barry, Head of Sustainable Business, M&S

Our culture both helps and sometimes can hinder us with Plan A; but either way it's crucial to the success of Plan A. The way things get done, our culture, is an unspoken part of the plan; for example, I sit on the 'How we do business' committee, which is made up of senior members of the business. The discussions are often on how to engage employees – what enablers and barriers there are and on the culture and mindset – rather than on specific technical policy detail.

Our culture is about doing things right and sometimes that is about compliance and sometimes about hierarchy. It means people are willing to work hard to deliver the written-down commitments of Plan A but it also means that it can be harder to get people to think of Plan A as a broader way of doing business, an opportunity for them to find their own ways to make the business more sustainable. For me, if you have the drive to build on the compliance culture then you can drive things forward. You need to be smart about showing people how – by pushing Plan A beyond compliance with the written commitments they can deliver better business outcomes for themselves, delight customers, motivate our people, become more efficient and open up new revenue streams. Where we've created this self-motivated culture we've seen step change – such as shwopping,[1] and our new Cheshire Oaks eco-store. With these success stories we can then also create internal competition to help excite other parts of the business to push Plan A, and that fits with our culture that is internally competitive and benchmark against each other.

Culture has always been important for transforming a business into a leading sustainable one. Twelve years ago I 'read' the organisation, focused on understanding it. We have a rich history of doing the right thing and this is really important but the problem back then was that the execution was not intentional, not strategic. There were lots of people doing the right thing in pockets around the organisation, but this lacked leadership. So with HR and senior directors we shepherded them together, connecting them. This was important, creating a reference point that employees could use to look at the organisation. We benchmarked ourselves and got stakeholder feedback and shared this with employees, as a way to hold up a mirror to the organisation so that we could really see who we were. We showed them best practice, and the positives such as awards, which slowly helped to build confidence. The Plan A branding that was then brought in was a reference point showing the totality of the business, showing the shared effort and the shared risks we were facing and taking. Plan A gave safety in numbers and encouraged employees to get involved; it accelerated the culture we were trying to build. It made sustainability feel important in a business with many change programmes and it gave us continuity, a reassuring sense of continuous improvement, not a 'flash in the pan' initiative.

Whoever is working on a sustainability programme needs to be culturally aware, and change awareness. This is essentially a big change programme. In everything we do we look at how to get things into the business, how to engage and work in the system of the business. All of my team work with HR as well, to understand how the business operates. It's about strategic change management!

I can't stress enough the importance of seeing a sustainability programme as a change programme. Ensuring that everyone is contributing to improving the social/environmental performance of every product, store, factory and raw material we use and that in doing so everyone can see the economic benefits that improvement brings.

Carmel McQuaid, Climate Change Manager Plan A, M&S (UK)

Overall, M&S is a really great place to work. M&S has a very strong culture, a definite way of getting things done. Some of this is for historic reasons; for example, we care very much about customer trust in the M&S brand – we feel a responsibility to live up to their expectations of our customers and therefore protect that reputation internally. This means we can be cautious with new ideas or products. Some of the way we do things is also because of how we are physically structured – with stores across the territories that focus on their areas and community; team loyalty can be first to that team rather than the wider employee base. We are all very loyal and proud of the M&S brand; this is important and reminds us of how we are expected to act.

The Plan A team recognised from the start that it was important to understand how things get done at M&S, how the system works. Some cultural aspects have been an advantage for us, such as the importance of external perception. This ongoing external scrutiny is helpful because it keeps our teams focused on finding solutions that can deliver our Plan A commitments. Also, our annual auditing process – where independent external auditors assess our achievements – is hugely helpful in ensuring delivery to Plan A remains a priority during busy day-to-day trading activity. The process we have for ideas or investment being approved at board level was also important to understand and capitalise on; the board has senior-level representation from different business functions and also has external input to proposals. This means that there is greater buy-in across the business before an approved project even starts – and that increases the chances of success.

However, some other cultural aspects have caused some problems. For example, the complexity of working across business and some cultural conservatism can make it difficult to introduce significant changes – especially when they impact on other parts of the business. To overcome this we set up the Innovation Fund, a protected pot of money that makes it clear we are looking for people to be brave and suggest new ways of doing things. So in this example we recognised a cultural barrier and put in place a mechanism for managing through that.

Another challenge in M&S Head Office is that personal networks are very strong and not always transparent. This makes it initially difficult for people who join from outside M&S. So getting buy-in and approval can be a very long process – further complicated by the workload that people are juggling which means time is always limited. Within the Plan A team we realised that we needed to have links into the various networks across the business – Plan A had to be leader-lead, people had to very visibly see that our CEO was serious about it. For example, Marc makes a point of taking an item to shwop when he is visiting a store.

It was also important to frame sustainability as an 'enabler' rather than another 'job to do'. For example, we created a Plan A champions network across the stores and this helps us to connect locally where there can be strong subcultures. We help champions get that little bit more from their job in their area, and they help with embedding Plan A locally as a business-wide objective. This, and providing initiatives for local teams to engage their community, is something the stores value. Plan A provides a lot of platforms for engaging employees, for ways that individuals can get involved and feel connected and motivated with M&S.

One feature that is particular to our Head Office culture is curiosity and a respect for external expertise. Our technical teams in particular are experts but we also bring specialists in to constructively challenge or validate what we are doing and demonstrate to our colleagues the external perception. So we find ways to work within the system, the culture. It does not mean the system is bad or good, but simply that we recognise it and figure out how to succeed in it.

Carmel's key areas of focus are defining what it means to be a truly sustainable retailer, integrating Plan A into products, working with farming supply base and supporting delivery of the business' climate change commitments. Prior to M&S she worked as a consultant for PA Consulting, having started her career as a chemical engineer in ICI.

1.2 Unsung Heroes

This chapter explores the case study of M&S in depth as an organisation that strategically engages employees to create a sustainable culture that then enables sustainable business success. Four stories are told at the start of this chapter of specific M&S employees doing just this. They are 'Unsung Heroes' because they quietly do this 'under the radar'; they work with others across the business in a manner that is not designed to draw overt recognition to the work they do in creating the engaging culture of M&S. This is not to hide their work – the organisation has given them dedicated roles to work on engagement and they are publicly recognised for other focus areas of their jobs – but because 'culture' can be sensitive, intangible and people can be very protective of 'how they do things'.

> Culture is an unspoken part of our plan. We don't have a dedicated 'culture' plan, or a tactical plan written up. A great strength is that we don't have it written down. But culture does affect how we do things, how we progress and it is something we look at strategically.
>
> (Mike Barry, M&S)

Thus, they are representative of the Unsung Heroes sitting within organisations helping to create organisational cultures that are enabling and responsible. Their effect is usually noticed when they are not present (i.e. cultures that do not enable sustainable success), but when they are present and when they succeed then 'the way things get done' becomes an asset and enables business success.

At M&S there are two teams involved in engagement and creating a sustainable culture:[2] the Engagement Team sitting in HR, and the Plan A team working on sustainable business. They work closely with each other and recognise and respect the benefits each team can bring to their own objectives. Research shows that the objectives of HR and a sustainability team often overlap and working together can be beneficial (Liebowitz, 2010). This is because sustainability is a good platform for creating an engaged workforce (Sirota *et al.*, 2005; Sirota Survey Intelligence, 2007), and pursuing sustainable objectives is greatly facilitated by having employees engaged in the business (Mirvis, 2012). Sadly, this close working relationship between sustainability teams and HR is not that common. However, at M&S this works well and together the two teams have created an engaged workforce and a culture where sustainable business has thrived.

1.3 Organisational culture

In October 2012 UBS London trader Kweku Adoboli was put on trial in the UK for fraud and false accounting – he was blamed for losses for the bank of £1.4 billion due to risky trades. Over the duration of his and his colleagues' testimony what emerged was not a clear story of a greedy man finally caught, but also of a loyal – if very misguided – employee who took bad actions because of pressure to deliver and because risk-taking was the culture of the bank.[3]

> Kweku Adoboli: UBS was my family and every single thing I did, every single bit of effort I put into that organisation, was for the benefit of the bank. That is everything I lived for.
>
> Compliance . . . a 'tick-box exercise' . . . the real message coming from senior managers . . . was that it was fine to bend the official rules to make a profit for the bank.
>
> (Neate, 2012)
>
> Charles Sherrard: The very nature of the bank became more aggressive in terms of its desire to make profit . . . The mantra coming from above was revenue, revenue, revenue.
>
> (Fortado and Moshinsky, 2012)

This and many other recent examples from the banking sector gives a glimpse into the culture of many banks and sectors of the finance industry that encourage a way of doing business that is risky and puts 'profit over people'. This specific 'way of doing business' seems to be so widespread that many within this system have lost perspective on what is acceptable societal behaviour and what is not. Not surprising, therefore, that in 2009 the then Head of the UK Financial Services regulator, Adair Turner, described much of the banking sector's activities as 'socially useless' (Inman, 2009).

Often called the 'corporate system', organisations seem to develop a unique 'way of getting things done' that almost develops a life of its own; encouraging a certain type of behaviour that becomes self-reinforcing. This can result in corporate success – or failure. This 'system' is the *organisational culture*. People work within that system, or culture, sometimes developing it, encouraging it, immersing themselves in it or trying to change it. Its existence is not as obvious as a physical asset, yet organisational culture is always present and having an effect on how employees act. When strategically managed, culture can be positive for both organisational and individual success (Lim, 1995); there is a strong relationship between an engaged workforce and financial success (Edmans, 2011), and evidence shows an association between strong performance socially and environmentally with financial performance (Orlitzky *et al.*, 2003). 'Culture' is especially relevant for sustainability because being responsible – at both an individual and organisational level – is personal, complex and context-specific. However, not many organisations approach the system – their culture – as a strategic asset and as a consequence negative cultures and bad consequences can arise – a likely contribution to Kweku Adoboli's actions at UBS.

So what is organisational culture? In 1982 academics Deal and Kennedy provided a simple definition of organisational culture:

The way things get done around here.

(Deal and Kennedy, 1982)

In other words, culture is the collective behaviour of those in the business that results in the way things get done. Why that behaviour happens – the motivation for the behaviour – is important for understanding why that behaviour emerges. Helpfully, further research has sought to define this concept further; academic Edward Schein is a well-recognised expert on organisational culture and has identified a *set of forces* that influence 'the way things get done' (Schein, 2010):

1. Regular behaviours when people interact, such as language used, customs and traditions and rituals
2. Group norms, such as standards and values
3. Espoused values, such as 'responsible'
4. The formal ideology principles and the policies that back these up and guide employee actions to stakeholders
5. Rules of the game: the unwritten rules for getting along, often emerged over time
6. Climate: the impact physical layout can have on how members of the organisation interact with each other
7. Embedded skills: specific competencies taught from one generation to the next
8. Habits: of thinking and mental models used that guide perceptions and language
9. Shared meaning: the emergent understandings that are created as group members interact with each other
10. Integrating symbols: how the group characterises itself and reinforces this visually, unconsciously or purposely, such as office layouts, logos and artefacts
11. Formal rituals and celebrations of key achievements and of how they reflect on important values.

These forces can be simplified further by clustering them into two groups:

1. *Behaviours,* whether as a result of carrying out embedded processes and procedures, everyday routine behaviours such as interaction, the habits of task achievement, formal rituals or policies that guide behaviour. Processes and procedures refer to the formal behaviours that are explicitly requested. Habits, routine behaviours, climate and rituals refer more to the informal (or shadow) behaviours,[4] such as the unspoken power

brokers, the political games, accepted normal behaviour in the wider regional context[5] and those habits of repetitive action (such as who you go to for advice) that form over time to become the norm.

2. *Motivation for those behaviours* that stem from the purpose or shared meaning employees want to create from their workplace, group norms which can be influenced by wider forces such as industry- and country-wide norms, espoused values of the organisations and therefore the motivation to act in a certain way, beliefs of individuals and how this affects their motivation, and operational motivational factors such as from ownership structure (e.g. pride in working for a co-op), historical context (e.g. an early leader who made responsibility core to the business, such as at Levi Strauss or Cadbury) or how reward and recognition are managed. Symbols used in the organisation can often represent these motivations.

Thus, culture can be described as 'a set of behaviours' driven by 'motivation for the enactment of those behaviours', which in turn reinforce and shape each other. This reinforcing influence creates a unique type of culture specific to each organisation.

It is important to understand the dominant culture from a holistic viewpoint – i.e. not just from one position or location in the organisation. Different employees will have different perspectives based on their rank, physical location, immediate department and position of responsibility of their specialism (subcultures). This is because an organisation is like an iceberg – only the very tip of the iceberg that is above the water line can be publicly seen[6] (Schein, 2010).

However, this definition can still seem 'vague' and 'fluffy' and not a tangible strategic asset – it is hard to identify and manage these forces as one would a physical asset, brand or set of accounts. Despite further academic research that has even created tools for diagnosing culture,[7] the idea of 'culture' can still be seen as irrelevant to everyday business decisions, precisely because it is about intangible motivations, actions, mindset and behaviours. It is hard to quantify, price and therefore put a monetary value on. But of course, as seen with example after example of rogue bankers and traders, and failed mergers and acquisitions,[8] culture is important precisely because it does guide the way things get done – and it is usually recognised when it does not work. What makes up culture therefore needs to be seen as 'structural mechanisms' dictating how things get done – such as a specific power structure, the language of the organisation, and agreed shared values and behaviours. Culture is a VRIN asset that needs to be strategically managed – 'Valuable, Rare, Inimitable, and Non-substitutable'.[9]

The culture of our business supports our ambitions . . . needs to be carefully managed.

(Sarah Findlater, M&S)

1.4 An engaged culture: a strategic asset for sustainable business

As a strategic asset, an organisation's culture is not necessarily 'good' or 'bad'; different organisations have different types of culture because the forces playing on them are different in characteristics. Therefore, the 'fit' of a culture to its context and strategic mission is very important; it is not accurate simply to identify and then define a culture as 'bad' or 'good'. Although many employees are – and data shows this trend increasing – attracted to organisations with 'engaged cultures'[10] (Net Impact, 2012), other organisational cultures focus dominantly on the financial success an employee can contribute and therefore offer a 'transactional' relationship (target achievement for a narrow set of rewards). An engaged culture is not necessarily 'better' than this transactional culture as the transactional culture may be suitable to its unique context – for example, it may work for people looking for a transactional relationship and motivated primarily by monetary reward. It may not work for an organisation that needs discretional behaviour, innovation and long-term commitment – but if this is not part of the strategic mission then the transactional culture may work. (However, when this particular type of transactional culture does not work it is often because it is not carefully managed.)

Nevertheless, when sustainable behaviour is embedded into the normal behaviour of a culture – i.e. not seen as separate, deviant behaviour – it significantly helps to create a sustainable culture (Ralston, 2009). And a sustainable culture is an asset that is proven to be positive for long-term business success. Academics Eccles, Ioannou and Serafeim showed in a 2011 Harvard Business School paper that companies with active sustainability-related cultural structural mechanisms for good governance, long-term thinking and better stakeholder engagement ('high sustainability companies') resulted in notably better long-term financial performance than 'low sustainability companies'. In which case, what does such a culture look like? And given that a large organisation can have subcultures that need to be considered (Frost *et al.*, 1991) (especially if located across different regions), are there particular characteristics that indicate and support the existence of a sustainable culture?

Cultures of organisations claiming to be sustainable have been assessed and some characteristics specific to sustainable organisations have been identified, such as:

- The personal values of managers being active (Duarte, 2010)
- A focus on reward and recognition, ability of the organisation to learn and manage change, awareness and involvement of employees in the business, employees able and welcomed to ask questions, problem identification and solving welcomed, respect for each other and stakeholders (Lyon, 2004)
- Values embedded in company practices, formalised processes for reporting sustainable performance, symbols present, such as slogans and

logos promoting values, a common language that is sculpted to include sustainability terminology and stories told that focus on sustainable successes (Duarte, 2011).

However, to date (in part because this is still a relatively new field in academia) these have not been compared across a wide group of companies to search for common characteristics, as has been done for (for example) entrepreneurial organisations (McGuire, 2003). Some common characteristics observed are detailed in Table 1.1, but this is not a robust meta-analysis, rather anecdotal evidence from the author's experience and case studies.

Even though some common characteristics have been observed, there is still not enough research to say that a particular culture type equates to having a sustainable culture and therefore a sustainable business. Further, the common enabling characteristics (in Table 1.1) often manifest in different ways in different organisations and so cannot yet be seen as ingredients for success. For example:

- An engaged workforce may mean employees engaged in being a member of the organisation because they are proud to be associated with the business – as seen with M&S – or could mean employees are motivated to achieve specific targets so that the organisation and individual maintain a reputation of success (and so are engaged in the reputation of the firm[11]). One or both of these could be the reason for an engaged workforce in any one organisation; they are not mutually exclusive. And both of these cited reasons can create positive and negative outcomes, dependent on a variety of other factors, such as a strong brand identity, respect for a wide group of stakeholders and long-term thinking.

The culture of M&S is described as traditional in processes, sometimes rigid or erring towards a compliance culture, having power networks and prone to silo thinking. On their own, this can seem to dissuade engagement or sustainable culture. But we know this not to be true at M&S, from their great success and testimony from employees of their pride and engagement in Plan A and the business. This is because these specific culture characteristics have positive outcomes as well, and when strategically managed together they create an engaged culture. For example:

- The cultural characteristic of 'doing the right thing' can create a degree of caution towards new ideas that first need to prove they fit this characteristic – even though 'innovation' is also a cultural characteristic. The business is very comfortable, indeed passionate, about innovating on what it knows well – better food or clothing – but it can be nervous about innovating in new areas, which is where they were with sustainability in 2007. These two characteristics can therefore sometimes pull in different directions and this has been circumvented by demonstrating

Table 1.1 Example common characteristics of a sustainable organisational culture

Influence on characteristics	Detail	Examples at M&S
History	A clear and accurate organisational identity Historical context that provides cultural characteristics relevant to sustainability, such as a pioneer, innovator, historically an organisation that engages with communities	M&S has a strong legacy of being a responsible business. This meant Plan A fitted well into the historical context of M&S. The brand is very well known in its main market, the UK, and this reputation is part of the organisational culture and is protected – this can sometimes cause hesitation about new ideas, but also robustness for new products having multiple layers of worth
Ownership	A shared set of espoused values and level of personal interaction of owners. Many companies have distant owners who do not engage in what the business does, merely how much it makes. Owners who take an interest and have long-term investments, such as many pension funds, can influence the culture Physical ownership structures, whether slight influence (initially a family-run business) or large influence (being a cop-op)	M&S is publicly owned, but attracts long-term as well as medium-term investors. It has a high degree of private investors, which means the business remains in touch with customers' needs and wants
Size	Geographic spread can influence the development of subcultures, although even across subcultures there can be a set of dominant characteristics Regional locations can influence culture, for example, because of environmental or political pressures, religion, country culture and country stage of development	M&S culture has changed from when store managers typically had just one team who worked a day shift and they could communicate easily with them. Now with longer opening hours, more part-time working and larger stores, the challenges of communicating with staff in store are more difficult and make communications between stores even more challenging
Technology	Processes and procedures that encourage innovation, ideas generation and conversation can encourage learning, being open to new ideas and opinions Knowledge sharing and story-telling technology can help	M&S works hard to be technologically innovative, with products and processes for the way it does business. Plan A has been a platform for encouraging this, and technological development is promoting a

Table 1.1 Continued

Influence on characteristics	Detail	Examples at M&S
	disseminate positive (or negative) behaviours	culture of innovation. See the M&S Engagement Hub, described later, as an example
Goals and objectives	Clearly espoused organisational agenda that promotes responsible business Objectives include an engaged culture and happy workforce	To counter the quarterly trading focus that is normal in retail, M&S set a long-term five-year plan with ambitious targets – this became known as Plan A. Additionally, the 'softer' objectives of M&S and objectives of Plan A are clearly communicated to employees and integrated into the corporate culture. Data from M&S, detailed below, shows the contribution these soft skills make to business objectives and therefore performance success
Context	Economic, market, industry, geographical and societal environments. For example, economic constraints can influence short-/long-term investments or how the organisation values action that creates longevity	M&S is a unique combination of a consumer brand and a retailer. The involvement in the specification and production of the products opens employees to a more holistic view of supply chain, and an understanding of how social and environmental contexts can influence delivery. This macro-level thinking is evident in many of the senior management mindsets and reflects into the dominant culture as a company with global context
People	Employees who are engaged in the business Clear organisational leaders who represent and advocate sustainable business	M&S' reputation, way of doing business and processes in recruitment and integration send a clear message of what is expected of people and what M&S gives its people – a true two-way relationship. This shapes the motivation of its people and in turn the behaviour they exhibit. M&S has strong organisational leaders who represent a strong culture and way of doing business

Note: To cluster common characteristics, academic Handy's factors that influence culture (Handy, 1993) have been used (left-hand column) and adapted to observations of sustainable cultures in both literature and M&S example.

through the Plan A business case that sustainability works, encouraging innovators to look for new opportunities, by bringing external experts in to challenge, and creating a central innovation fund to encourage risk taking.

- The existence of silo thinking is a strength as it encourages loyalty to local colleagues and therefore contributes to local engagement and so is a positive characteristic. Rather than discourage this, the M&S Unsung Heroes focus on also creating opportunities for teams to engage with other parts of the business so that wider team thinking can emerge (the 'In Touch' approach).

> In Touch: One united team working collaboratively and efficiently with common ways of working and clear communication.
>
> (M&S internal guidance document for In Touch)

Further, other cultural characteristics exist that more clearly encourage a culture of engagement and sustainability, such as pride in the brand, knowing the organisation will always do the right thing, being bold in taking leaps of faith when it made sense and the business case is proven and being very respectful of what customers and employees expect from M&S (as a brand).

Therefore, what seems to be important is *how* the Unsung Heroes – those managing the culture as a strategic asset – understand the cultural characteristics and work within, bypass or manipulate such cultural characteristics. What seems to be important is understanding the culture as an asset to be strategically managed, capitalising on these strengths and managing the characteristics that can make things more difficult – just as one would for any other strategic organisational asset.

> Our culture is critical for how things get done. It influences our success and we have to be strategic with understanding it.
>
> (Mike Barry, M&S)

1.5 Advice for Unsung Heroes

The critical advice for Unsung Heroes is to understand the organisational context – the organisational culture for engaging employees – as an asset and assign resources accordingly.

1.5.1 Know your organisation's culture

What is clear from the M&S case study is how important it is for Unsung Heroes to understand what their organisational culture looks like. As previously discussed, this is not to pass judgement on what is 'good' or 'bad', but to understand the parameters to work within. A useful tool for this is the Culture Web, developed in 1992 (and updated in 2005) by academics

Johnson and Scholes. The Culture Web is a tool that can be used to view the artefacts of the organisation (the symbols and symptoms visible). Six specific dimensions are used to do this (Figure 1.1).

1.   Stories: the past events that employees talk about inside and outside the organisation. Who and what the company chooses to 'immortalise' can represent cultural values and perceptions of behaviour.
2.   Rituals and routines: the daily behaviour and interactions of employees that represent acceptable behaviour. This guides what is expected to happen in given situations.
3.   Symbols: the visual representations of the organisation, including logos, office decor and formal or informal dress codes.
4.   Organisational structures: the structure defined by an organisation chart, and also the unwritten lines of power and influence that represent whose contributions are most valued.
5.   Control systems: the ways that the organisation is controlled, such as the financial systems, quality systems and rewards.

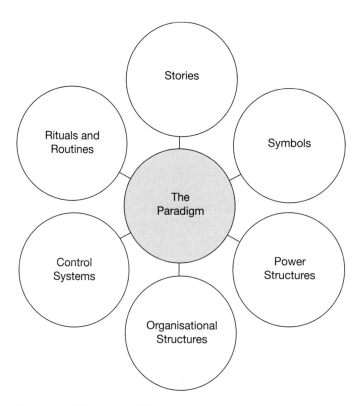

Figure 1.1 The Culture Web.

Source: Johnson and Scholes (2005).

6. Power structures: who (and where) the real power exists in the organisation. This could be restricted to one or two key senior executives, a whole group of executives or even a department.

Each element looks at the conscious and (importantly) the unconscious elements of the organisation. For example, Stories looks at the type of stories told informally (the 'watercooler' stories) in comparison with those told formally via legitimate platforms (internal newsletter). Utilising this Culture Web as a diagnostic tool can help uncover what the real culture of the organisation is. This can help Unsung Heroes to formulate a strategic approach to engaging employees for a sustainable culture and invest in tactics and resources relevant to the organisation's unique culture for success.

For example, at M&S the Plan A team identifies and looks for opportunities to 'nudge'[12] the culture in a new direction. The new CEO and leadership team (new in 2010–11) combined with a change of head office location and offices decoration have specifically changed power structures, rituals and routines, and symbols. These changes have given the Plan A team a platform to introduce the idea of change into the cultural mindset that will help with both scaling up of the business and driving a shift in strategy as more ambitious targets are set.

1.5.2 Understand the cultural characteristics for engaging employees in sustainability

When one understands the organisational culture, it is then helpful to understand how the unique characteristics of that culture influence behaviours and motivations specifically for sustainable success. A 2011 guide of how to engage employees in sustainability provides a four-step audit that Unsung Heroes can undertake to identify their cultural characteristics for engaging employees specifically in sustainability (Exter, 2011). As a summary, it is critical to identify specific cultural *characteristics* and how they manifest as enablers or barriers. This is not to pass judgement on the organisation, but to understand context and identify a plan of action specific to the organisation's context and culture. Example enablers and barriers are summarised in Table 1.2.

1.5.3 Work with the business, not against it

The Unsung Heroes at M&S are good examples of a team who understand that culture is an asset, that the specific cultural characteristics of their organisation are enablers or barriers for sustainable success and how to work within that business context rather than against it.

The M&S HR and Plan A team recognised that they needed to talk the language of business – of sales and profitability – to get people's attention. They have the business acumen and the understanding of how 'things get

Table 1.2 Examples of cultural barriers and enablers for engaging employees in sustainability

Barrier	Why a problem
Employees are uninterested in sustainability	Preparatory work needs to be done that may relate to the culture of the organisation and something you are not able to change (due to power, resources or authority)
Employees work in a 'heads-down' culture, protecting their own area (whether own job or silos of departments)	A culture of protection implies barriers to entry to certain areas of the business, which may be critical in delivering sustainability targets and solutions
Projects and spend driven only by short-/mid-term financial returns	Some sustainability spend is based on 'leaps of faith' or longer-term returns, which are hard to accept in a culture of short-termism but essential to undertake
Significant command and control system in place	Lack of empowerment means it will be hard for individuals to feel they are allowed to take on additional roles, and rewarding them will be difficult as it could be seen as 'depowering' those with existing authority
Sustainability team has no authority or is positionally irrelevant	It will be hard to build trust in their competence and persuade people to get involved in projects, and could be hard to have successful communication with employees
No clear values or ethics of the organisation, as understood by employees	This makes it hard to rationalise efforts with the values of the organisation, and you will need to focus on individual motivation for activities, and mainly on the business case for sustainability
No clear, or a weak, sustainability strategy	Without strong direction and communication, the goal and therefore the reason for a project, activity, mindset or spend is not clear
Lack of leadership skills for sustainable business	The skills for leading a sustainable business (whether leaders or the Sustainability Specialists) include relationship building, cross-function perspective, having an external perspective and a strong sense of purpose. Lack of these skills will make it hard to 'get it right' and deliver results
Leaders do not support sustainability efforts	If leaders are not supportive, why should employees be?
Enabler	Why powerful
Employees are engaged in the business	The culture empowers you to introduce sustainability to the workforce, focusing on why, benefits and how it supports the business – not on deep cultural change

Table 1.2 Continued

Employees are already interested in specific elements of sustainability	A way to capitalise on existing interest in how employees make sense of sustainability, and a way to build champions from a defined area of the business
Leaders want to drive the organisation to be more responsible and sustainable	Leadership support and tone from the top are critical as they signal permission for employees to get involved, signal expectation that sustainability is relevant to business success and hint at 'power' or reputational gains for individuals who get involved
The Specialist team has good existing relationships with key leaders and managers	A way in, allies to work with, and so being able to sense-check and initiate a cascade effect throughout the organisation
Other initiatives (not sustainability-related) that were cross-organisation have been successful	Existing routes across the business to use, employees understand the need and practicality of working with other departments and employees understand the business is one linked organisation
A strong and relevant sustainability strategy (even if not communicated yet)	A good platform relevant to the business will resonate well with employees and provide opportunities for collaboration and synergies with business drivers
Clear, relevant organisational values	A good platform to start from, which, if relevant to the business, will resonate well with employees and provide opportunities for collaboration and synergies with business drivers
Related systems in place already (e.g. knowledge capturing, personal appraisals)	Existing expectations of how the business works will not block other sustainability-related measures being integrated. Existing routes into the business for you to utilise

done' at M&S and how to work the system so that the business can understand the contribution an engaged workforce gives to financial success.

As described earlier, M&S has a cultural characteristic of taking initial leaps of faith if an idea sounds sensible – and so HR decided to collate hard data on the difference engaged employees made to the business. Initial engagement scores were collated by the HR team and provided the ammunition for that leap of faith to be taken. When the initial data was presented to senior directors at M&S (Your Say survey), a decision was made that engagement needed a dedicated department, with a Centre of Excellence. This sort of recognition and focus sends a clear message to the employee base that this approach is important to the business – it provided legitimacy and credibility within the business that helped specifically with working through the cultural characteristic of 'difficulty in gaining access to the internal decision-makers' (Bansal, 2003).

The M&S Engagement team collate both the 'hard' and 'soft' data and actively share it with the business, providing both financial impact and personal stories and quotes. This combination of both types of data ('hard' and 'soft') gets the attention of a broad base of employees. By further providing examples, ideas, skills training, reading and advice, the Engagement team can turn that attention into action by helping managers to understand tangible actions they can take. The 'intangible' becomes tangible. Example advice given is:

> *Small things, BIG IMPACT: Make time for recognition, whether it's straightforward thank-yous or through spending every penny of your Spotlight Awards.*

This combination of hard and soft data is representative of what motivates M&S employees to act – they value the 'gut' feeling that something is right to do, but swiftly follow this up with hard data to give the idea longevity, and then get 'real-world' advice from the Unsung Heroes.

Legitimacy is also an important enabler to build. This can be legitimacy as a member of the organisation or your team (where newer members need to build up credibility of their place and contribution to the business), as a change-maker (especially in relation to representing an organisational priority, and in individual reputation for being an effective change-maker), as a power broker (if the organisation is one where power and authority drive decision-making) or as relevant to the organisation (speaks in the language of the organisation and operates within the accepted norms of behaviour). For example, understanding how to talk with colleagues – using familiar and accepted language and themes as a way of capturing their attention (Whitehouse, 2006). Sometimes, managers focus only on what they perceive to be on the corporate agenda – what is permissible to address – and so getting senior and respected members of the organisation (such as a Godparent; see Chapter 5) talking about the importance of engaging employees in sustainability can help reinforce the message that sustainable business is on that agenda (Bansal, 2003), which in turn encourages employees to be open to what Unsung Heroes do.

1.5.4 Invest wisely

Resources are usually constantly restricted and it is important to show the benefits of engagement to the business. Likewise, it is important to consider how Engagement and Sustainability teams can work together to maximise impact whilst managing resources well. Over the past five years the Plan A team have recognised that specific cultural characteristics within M&S could both help and hinder the transformational change programme they were initiating and so invested in a person responsible for engaging employees (the People strategy). When they reviewed this role through a strategic lens, using business objectives such as criteria, it became clear the People strategy was about engaging employees. They therefore worked with HR to coordinate efforts and the person responsible – Sophie – now sits within HR, working closely with both teams and making better use of resources and organisational structures and positioning.

Sophie – the employee wholly dedicated to engaging employees through Plan A – and the Engagement team quantify their objectives for investing specifically in engaging employees through Plan A. They link specific tactics to overarching business objectives and clearly show the business case. For example, a specific set of key benefits has been identified (such as 'driving employer brand', 'driving engagement levels' and 'raising the profile of retail as a career') and each initiative is linked to one of these benefits. The M&S Retail Ambassador Programme, for example – where employees act as retail ambassadors in schools – supports the business benefit of 'raising the profile of retail as a career'.

The Marks & Start programme is a good example of an investment in what initially seemed to give 'soft' returns but has generated multiple levels of benefits. When M&S first launched Marks & Start it was a leap of faith that it would help engagement and in turn help productivity. M&S take a lot of leaps of faith but then follow that up with assessing the success – proving the success, which is what they did for Marks & Start.

> Marks & Start really scores well for driving engagement and generating passion and pride in our employees. There are also great business benefits, for example with recruitment. We have a pool of trained people waiting for a job at peak times. This Christmas [2012] we have about 700 people available to work for us. This is an obvious business benefit, but importantly the social impact of the programme really engages our employees working with or near the placement person; they can see the person grow and develop and be proud of being part of that change.
>
> (Sophie Brooks, Plan A Employee Engagement)

> The Marks & Start programme is a good example of a successful initiative that links impact with business benefits. It has had significant 'soft' impact on engagement, pride, skills development, and identity reinforcement; and 'hard' business impact on recruitment in peak times and retention rates.
>
> (Eve Chamberlain, Marks & Start Coordinator, Brighton Store)

At an individual level, understanding what the overarching business objectives and priorities are – and how your plans are related to and support this agenda (Bansal, 2003) – can help clearly articulate the business case and 'legitimise' the soft benefits or investment leaps of faith.

1.6 Advice for organisations

The academic research into culture as a corporate asset is well established and continuing research is further linking sustainable businesses with engaged employees. However, outside academia the approach of managing culture as a specific asset (and actively linking this with sustainability performance) is still in its early stages. A few leading companies do have employee engagement teams and/or sustainability teams, and in some of these best-practice examples the teams work together – as seen at M&S – but this is still unusual. If teams or individuals are resourced and given the responsibility, access, power and legitimacy to focus on engaging employees and creating an engaged, responsible culture, then this can be the single biggest enabler that leaders of the organisation can give Unsung Heroes for creating a workforce engaged in sustainable business.

1.6.1 How to be strategic: recognise an engaged culture is an asset

Sarah spoke of the growing understanding within M&S over a period of time of how important an engaged workforce is to business success. This started with her team collating evidence from 2007, in the form of a yearly employee survey (Your Say) covering questions about engagement (employees feeling informed, proud, advocates, able to express ideas), job satisfaction, motivation and happiness. Year on year the engagement scores within that survey were enlightening: stores with higher than average business performances also had higher than average engagement scores. In 2011 they introduced a shorter engagement survey which is completed quarterly (called Pulse) and in April 2012 the Engagement team published hard data internally showing that:[13]

- Stores with the highest engagement scores (averaging six percentage points higher than the average) can achieve over 10% higher profitability.

The team also share 'soft' data:

> I've always been a huge advocate of employee engagement because during my management career I've seen the difference it makes time after time.
> (Dave Bruce, M&S Store Manager Kensington, London[14])

This data is a strong business case for engaging employees, and it is no surprise that the Engagement team have – in the last 2 years especially – received strong interest from store managers and senior directors on how to improve the culture of engagement as an asset to their area of the business.

Likewise, the Plan A team have been strategic with how they approach engaging employees, with 'Engaging Employees' being a commitment in Plan A and with a target date of 2012 whereby they had to have achieved some degree of engagement in Plan A with every employee (this was achieved). Engaging employees has been beneficial for the Plan A team, both in helping with the area of Plan A commitments around being a responsible employer and also because an engaged culture further enables sustainable business to be embedded.[15] The team identified three levels of business priority ambitions in relation to their strategy for 'People' in Plan A:

1. Those that they want to develop and be competitive with in performance
2. Those they want to be industry leaders in
3. Those they want to be world class in.

As well as prioritising efforts (and therefore time and resource), this approach also links outcomes with business-wide objectives and sets clear and ambitious targets that can be used to interest managers and directors.

The Plan A team likewise have a strategy for how they create a culture of innovation for sustainability and how they integrate Plan A into the 'processes and procedures' of M&S (a key element of how culture is maintained).

1.6.2 Lever points for managing culture

Research by academic Professor Liebowitz on the role of HR and organisational culture has identified some 'levers' that can be utilised to achieve a sustainable culture (Liebowitz, 2010). He identified 12 levers that HR have power to manage: recruitment, employee selection, new employee orientation, training and development, performance management, compensation, empowerment, job security, succession planning, mentoring, innovation and collaboration. For example:

• Recruitment: Professor Liebowitz advocates HR looking first internally when recruiting, for example to build trust from employees that the organisation recognises the assets it has, is fair and provides equal opportunities. Job descriptions providing expected attributes can help with integration and create a wider shift within the employee base as new employees with responsible mindsets join the organisation – such as asking for attributes of team work and caring for the environment. Additionally, if companies actively recruit from MBA programmes with a clear sustainability track, this helps attract employees who may fit better with or help create a sustainable culture (see Chapter 5, Godparents, for an example of this).

Academics Willcoxson and Millet (2000) identify a further five levers:

1. Socialisation of new employees but also for existing employees moving up the hierarchy. 'Development and training can provide for acculturation to an existing or new culture.'

2. Leadership and modelling by senior managers and directors can reinforce or help change existing myths, symbols, behaviour and values, and 'demonstrates the universality and integrity of vision, mission or value statements'.
3. Participation of all employees in cultural activities or maintenance gatherings, because being part of decision-making and development helps employees to buy into and even own long-term change in values and behaviours.
4. Interpersonal communication: satisfying interpersonal relationships can support an existing culture and integrate employees (reinforced by a common language, form of communication, visual effects used and tone of communications); effective teamwork also supports the development of an engaged culture.
5. Structures, policies and procedures and allocation of resources (described earlier as both causes and expressions of behaviours), which need to support the desired organisational culture and objectives.

1.6.3 Tactical actions

The team at M&S have developed specific tools and tactics to help them create a culture where employees are engaged. An internal web-based 'hub' was built as a portal specifically for line managers of all levels and employee representatives (called 'Big' groups) to access to learn more, be informed, trained or get involved in creating an engaged culture. Called the Engagement Hub, this resource was created by Sarah and her team to provide all types of advice, training and interaction points, whatever level of interest the reader has in employee engagement. Notably, they provide for three levels of interest: those with 5 minutes, 20 minutes or 1 hour to give to learning more about engagement. Sarah described the success of the hub due to three characteristics: it is flexible, practical and based on real-life M&S stories (Figure 1.2).

Many other organisations who have Unsung Heroes working on creating an engaged culture also develop such portals, but the flexibility of the M&S platform allows all types of employees to be interested, and above informing, it provides opportunities for learning and two-way interaction.

Additionally, the team develop other tools targeted at specific management-level employees to stay informed and educated and be taught the skills they need for engaging their departments.

- A quarterly booklet specifically for store and line managers focuses on informing and educating them of upcoming People activity, such as the Pulse survey, upcoming learning modules, an actions checklist and information on specific issues, such as changes to pension plans (We are M&S: People Quarterly)
- Unusually, the engagement team are also developing a booklet, mainly for newer employees, that articulates the culture of M&S. Similar to a

Figure 1.2 M&S Engagement Hub.

brand book developed by marketers for a brand (representing the brand characteristics and identity), the booklet will capture real characteristics of the culture and describe how this works. For example, in December 2012 in development was the phraseology to describe the pride employees have because they work at M&S and the reciprocal relationship of the effort they put in which continues to keep M&S special.

Specific initiatives can be powerful engagement tools whilst also delivering a business benefit. The previously mentioned Marks & Start is a good example of this, as a tool to engage existing staff in Plan A, increase engagement in the business (focusing specifically on pride, team identity and skills development) and delivering 'hard' benefits of recruitment, training of new staff and operational stability in peak times (Box 1.1).

The extent of professionalisation of the Engagement and Plan A teams at M&S is possible because the leadership view an engaged workforce in a sustainable business as critical to long-term business success. Both the previous and current CEOs advocate sustainable business and the importance of looking after their employees and doing business in a responsible way. This responsible leadership – and the tactics of the Unsung Heroes to gather the evidence, identify and then work within the cultural characteristics of M&S,

Box 1.1 Case study of an engagement tool with multiple benefits: Marks & Start

Panida is a single parent to three children. She has been a single parent for eight years. Panida had been out of work for four years and struggled with low confidence, but the Marks & Start course helped her realise the skills she had to give in the workplace. Panida received excellent feedback while on her placement and is now working in the food department at Cheshire Oaks. She says the Marks & Start course made her realise she's 'just as good as anyone else'.

I'd been unemployed for four years before I heard about the Marks & Start course. I'd been on income support, and then jobseeker's allowance. Childcare was always the big issue for me. Hours were a massive problem – there'd be jobs going but I couldn't take them because they needed people to work late hours or really early mornings which I couldn't do, because I'm a single parent and need to be there for my kids.

The Jobcentre told me that there was a course going for single parents called Marks & Start which helped you with your interview skills and helped you get your confidence back up. I wanted to do anything which would help get me back on the job market. So I put my name forward. I'd heard about the new store M&S were opening – the Cheshire Oaks store. I'd put my name down there almost a year before it opened I was that keen!

The Jobcentre put me in touch with Laura at Gingerbread [M&S charity partner for the initiative] who talked to me about going on the course and what it would be like – she was really helpful. We did three days of training with Gingerbread on things like interview techniques. It felt a bit like going back to school! When you've been out of touch for so long, it's really nice to see that there are other people like you – it really puts you at ease. You can see where you stand a lot better. It was also really good to be using my brain again. When you've been at home for a while with your kids, it's really good to have adult company and conversation again.

I did my work experience placement at the Heswall store. It was fantastic, I absolutely loved it. I really wanted to work in the food department, and Heswall is mostly food so that was perfect for me. I worked on the shop floor and then also on the operations side of things, in the stock room. You can't get such a good feel for a place only working in one area so it was really good to be able to move around and try new things, I learned loads. And everyone there was brilliant – my buddy Steve made sure I was OK.

After I finished my work placement, my supervisor told me they'd been really impressed with me and suggested I go for a job opportunity in Birkenhead. The same day, Laura from Gingerbread rang up to tell me there was an opportunity for me at the new Cheshire Oaks store. The Cheshire Oaks store is only two minutes down the road from me, so I went for that one and got the job!

I work in the food department and really love it. I think it's because I'm a bit of a foodie! But I also enjoy the interaction with the customers, especially the older customers. I like the M&S way of thinking that nothing's too much trouble – at times I'm like a personal shopper! I love doing it, making sure I'm helping as much as possible and it's my way of giving something back.

My shifts are really good. I work 7am to 12pm, so I'm there to pick up my youngest daughter from school every day. The kids can see I'm much happier now I'm working. I've got my independence back. I feel better within myself and I'm 100-fold more confident. I know now that I'm just as good as anyone else.

Louise Cassidy, HR Business Partner for Cheshire Oaks, where Panida now works

When we opened the new Cheshire Oaks store we recruited 33 candidates who had completed Marks & Start placements in local stores. At the start of the project we were really excited to work with the Marks & Start charity partners to give individuals from disadvantaged backgrounds the opportunity of employment at the new store. The individuals who secured a job at Cheshire Oaks were immensely proud of their achievement and were really excited by their new challenge. The programme had huge benefits for the store; we had a group of individuals who were really passionate and motivated about working for Marks & Spencer; it also allowed us to forge strong links in the local community. At Cheshire Oaks we have seen how Marks & Start can make a real difference to people's lives by giving them an opportunity. We are now looking forward to supporting the individuals who joined us through Marks & Start to be buddies for future programmes or pursue their aspirations through our career path.

Source: Case study provided by M&S (2012).

build the business case and manage their resources well – results in an organisational culture that is strong, unique and (despite some small frustrations) works well for M&S.

1.7 Concluding thoughts

A shift is occurring in the perception organisations have of the role of employees as value-creators, and specifically that how employees are able to 'get things done' is a critical and valuable asset to be strategically managed. Discussion around valuing human capital as an asset on the balance sheet is ongoing and a few leading companies do undertake this practice: Infosys is one such example and has placed a value on its entire workforce since 2008. This is included in the company balance sheet as an intangible asset alongside other 'intangibles' such as intellectual property assets (Kaye, 2012). An increasing number of academic studies are simultaneously showing the positive influence sustainable business has on employees (such as enhancing organisation justice, identification, social identity, trust, commitment, job satisfaction and actual behaviours: Gond *et al.*, 2010) and the effect on the performance of companies (Eccles *et al.*, 2011).

The HR profession has a critical role in this debate, and improving practice requires that the HR team in a company is seen (and skilled and resourced accordingly) as a strategic business enabler rather than just a team performing functional tasks such as posting recruitment adverts, following legislative updates and assisting in reviews. Likewise, the sustainability profession is critical in this debate because the link between sustainable business, an engaged workforce and enhanced business performance is now so clearly evident (Orlitzky *et al.*, 2003).

There are employees within a few leading organisations who have championed a strategic approach to managing culture, engaging employees and connecting this with transforming into a sustainable business. These Unsung Heroes have made a significant contribution to success by creating the context where employees engaged in sustainability can flourish. The following chapters chronicle the stories of four different types of extraordinary employees who are very engaged with their organisations and sustainable business and are having a significant positive impact. Their successes are explored, but what becomes clear from their stories is how critical the culture of their organisation is in enabling them to take action for sustainability. And so, as we celebrate their achievements, it is worth remembering the Unsung Heroes working in the background facilitating those successes.

> A business will not become sustainable unless it engages its entire workforce in change. There are simply too many moving bits of the 'machine' for a central team to change alone. Every product, store, factory, farm, raw material must be fundamentally better environmentally and socially in the not too distant future. Creating a culture that collectively embraces

sustainable change and sees the positive commercial opportunities that spin out of it is the only way forward.

(Mike Barry, M&S)

1.7.1 Summary advice

- An understanding of what one's unique organisational culture is, the forces that shape it and its contribution to business success can help to uncover a strategic and valuable inherent organisational asset.
- The HR and Sustainability teams can benefit from working with each other. This is helped if both teams are strategic in approach, rather than just tactical. Have frank and constructive discussions about where objectives and priorities match and if resources or initiatives can be shared for better effect, resource use and sharing of expertise.
- HR teams can benefit in their work if the organisational culture has sustainability-related characteristics as this can help to engage employees, and an engaged employee base can be a great asset to any business. Correspondingly, the Sustainability Specialists may benefit from working closely with HR in many instances, because a workforce engaged in the business enables change programmes for sustainability to be more easily embedded.
- The right skills and people to identify your culture and further uncover your organisation's unique characteristics can help identify the enablers and barriers to engaging employees in sustainable business. Those involved should try not to judge characteristics as 'good' or 'bad' (unless there are some very obvious negatives), but find the positive outcomes there are, or can be, and explore how to work within these parameters for success.
- Also recognise the importance of baseline metrics so that improvements in engagement can be tracked along the journey and with improvements in performance. This can help to reinforce the business case and interest more and more employees if they can view engagement as an enabler.
- If a programme to engage employees is initiated, look to change management tactics for advice. Work with the business and focus initially on areas that obviously support the corporate agenda as this can build relevance and support. Leaders should support this team.
- There are specific cultural characteristics which may help if they are further developed, and there are specific lever points that can be used to create an engaged culture. The power to use these may sit within the HR or sustainability teams.
- An understanding of the 'soft' and 'hard' outcomes from engaging employees can help to build enough of a business case to continue investing in developing an engaged culture. Look at how the initiatives can provide both 'soft' and 'hard' outcomes.
- Purposely move sustainability language, mindset and behaviour from unusual (deviant) behaviour into normal behaviour, for example by

embedding targets into all employees' key performance indicators and objectives, ensuring sustainable business is clearly on the espoused agendas of leaders and the organisation, and encouraging employees to talk about sustainability-related issues – in other words, engage employees in sustainable business, in your business!

1.8 Further reading

Hofstede G (1984). *Culture's Consequences: International Differences in Work-Related Values,* 2nd edn. Beverly Hills, CA: Sage.

Houchin K, MacLean D (2005). Complexity theory and strategic change; an empirically informed critique. *British Journal of Management* 16: 149–166.

Johnson G, Scholes K (2005). *Exploring Corporate Strategy,* 6th edn. London: Prentice Hall.

Weber Y (1996). Corporate cultural fit and performance in mergers and acquisitions. *Human Relations* 49 (9): 1181–1202.

2 The corporate Sustainability Specialist

Specialist: (noun) a person highly skilled in a specific and restricted field; (adjective) Possessing or involving detailed knowledge or study of a restricted topic.

It is a privilege to introduce some very unique and interesting people. Part of a relatively new profession, these are the corporate Sustainability *Specialists* – those within business who in their jobs focus solely on helping to change their organisation into a more responsible and sustainable one. Emerging from roles such as Community Manager and Health and Safety Manager, the corporate Sustainability Specialist is one of the newest business professional roles but is growing fast. It has changed significantly over the last decade to be one with significant professionalism, challenges, skills and impact.

The first part of this chapter chronicles the stories of some of these professionals. They briefly share their life history as it is only through following their journey and the interaction they have with the world that we can see how they have become the successful specialists they are today. The second part of the chapter explores the skills, competencies and motivations of a typical Specialist, and then gives advice on how this professional can be encouraged and enabled. The examples included here are their stories – honest, insightful and extraordinary. They show people with passion and drive, intellectual curiosity, a clear sense of self and identity and the ability to see the interconnectivity of individual action, business success and impact with the wellbeing of society and environment.

2.1 Case studies

Lynnette McIntire, Director of Sustainability, UPS (USA)

To thine own self be true, right? I think this holds true – I have a different way of thinking because I'm an ex-journalist, I am fascinated by and curious about issues and challenges and so I

> *question things a lot. I think over time this has been my greatest value to UPS – and they listen to me. I am making a difference here; I am being a change agent. It's dynamic, fascinating!*

I was born and grew up in Kentucky, USA, a typical blue-collar mid-sized town, in the late '60s and '70s. A lot of the civil rights movement, the Vietnam war, racial issues and women's issues were all at the forefront when I was growing up. I think that that was part of a social awareness that directly touched me to have connections with social issues that have now become sustainability issues. My parents were both teachers and I was always involved very much in community activities, church and as a young Democrat.

I always knew I wanted to be a journalist. It was a sense of social consciousness and being part of change really because I always viewed journalism as a noble profession that put a spotlight on social problems and issues. I also knew I was a good writer and so at 16 I started working for a radio station in the news department, one of only two women who had ever been on the air. The station general manager became a mentor to me and encouraged me to go to university to study journalism. After university I became a journalist, working on the Mississippi Bureau. I covered things like prison reform, extreme poverty and voters' rights. I was really lucky in that at the time I was covering a federal court with Judge William Keady[1] who was one of the civil rights federal judges that set a lot of precedents during that period. I started writing business news at the Memphis office and agriculture is obviously a big part of the economy in that area. Farming connects with the environmental side of sustainability and I saw first-hand the impact of things like cotton farming and agriculture. Everything was fascinating and I do think that being a journalist you are predisposed to being intellectually curious, to be curious about what's going on in the world and see how things are interconnected and what the impact and implications are.

I think most journalists come to a turning point when they have to decide if they want to make money for a living or just want to be in journalism. When I got married we moved to Minnesota and there was a job with a PR [public relations] agency – I was a bit apprehensive leaving the noble profession of journalism but they were interested in my skills. So I started working on a FedEx account and this got me interested in logistics. My job was to understand something, a situation, and then communicate about it, getting more into business models, world trade and understanding market place dynamics – which I find fascinating. And then a career opportunity arose within the PR agency to go to Bangkok. I had always wanted to go.

I was in Asia for about five years: two years in Bangkok agency side and then three years in Singapore where I worked for FedEx. Back then FedEx had a really good reputation and they were extremely fast moving. This is when the whole internationalisation of logistics and express transportation and all of that was happening. The FedEx Asia offices were only just being developed and there were only four of us in the office in Asia when I first started. I really like supply chain management and logistics and I was starting on the ground floor, seeing the world, and I really liked the people that I was working with. Also, they needed the skill set I had – it was a really great opportunity to make a huge difference in a short period of time. Asia in particular during that time was undergoing an economic boom. I got to understand what global trade was about, understand the bottom of the pyramid.[2]

A lot of the work I did was evaluating social projects that were relevant for multinationals to support and so I spent some time checking out local projects that helped people who lived on landfills and in slums. Just seeing the disparity between rich and poor and how economic development and world trade could have a positive impact on economic conditions . . . I think that kind of enlightenment is invaluable. In the sustainability space you see environmental disasters, you see what effect bad workplace safety can have. I remember tours in Bangkok, and when I asked why children are in hammocks in the slums and found out the reason is because it protects them from the rats, from rat bites . . . those kind of things stick with you. When you see children who have never been off the landfill in their lifetime and they are five years old and they spend their days picking through to try to find pieces of aluminum foil and copper wiring . . . it sticks with you. It's the kind of a situation where you start to say, okay what difference can I personally make and then what difference can I make using the resources of the clients or the employers that I have to make a difference. You ask yourself, 'How am I connected with the rest of the world?'

However, after five years I moved States-side again. I really felt like it was time to go home so I came back to Atlanta, where my family were. I do miss the buzz and being in the centre of the universe in Asia, but family came first. Eventually I ended up at UPS. UPS is a very well-respected company with a reputation for being very ethical. I always want to find a company where their values align with my own. I definitely feel that here, not just by what they say about themselves but how they are ranked and how employees talk about them. The company has a very unique culture of integrity and being good at working in the community.

And it was a dynamic time! I actually came to UPS to work on their entrepreneurial wing, the supply chain management unit – a separate new unit we had to build up. I got involved in a variety of projects – all the things that you would do in a smaller company. It felt a lot like when FedEx were getting started with four of us in the office in Asia. There was a lot of flexibility in what I did because I was growing the role as the unit grew. I became an integral part of the team and I helped shape that team.

And then I moved to the corporate office, to a position called 'Global Reputation'. I was a bit sceptical because historically that role had been about what is typically called the soft side and I was from the heavy-duty business side. But when I got into it I realised that there was a lot of issues management and that sustainability was coming up at the same time. There were a lot more reputational scorecards where we were not necessarily being represented well. I realised this is quite an opportunity for UPS because we actually were doing a lot of the right things.

In 2002 there was a small ad hoc group of people who just sort of came together on our own. There was somebody from environmental affairs, HR, operations and someone who is now our CFO [Chief Financial Officer], so he was an early champion of sustainability. We decided that a sustainability report was a good idea. Because of what UPS already did we could pretty much sail through rankings and got a lot of awards and top scores because nobody else was doing it. But as time went by and standards got more stringent, our scores kept dropping. We reached a turning point where we all said, as a group, that if we were going to move to the next phase we were going to have to do more, get much more support, because we are going to have to challenge things.

So as a group we all took certain issues – like the carbon disclosure project, the Dow Jones Sustainability Index – up through our chains of command. We went to the very top of the company and said that they all needed to get more involved in this because a lot of the things that will need to be done in the future have to be cross-functional with strategic decisions made from the top of the company. And they agreed! They appointed a member of the management committee to help us figure out what we needed to make this happen and he championed it from then on. As a group we made recommendations about how to set up a governance and reporting structure. We had a working committee which represented the 'worker bees' – the people who actually had to execute on these plans. We started out with maybe five or six functions and now it's a group of about 40 people.

I know UPS is a huge company but I am making a difference here, I am being a change agent. My job gives me permission to ask questions and say, 'Why aren't we reporting on this?' or 'Guess what, in the new world we need to re-evaluate what we are doing'. I can raise those issues as an individual. They don't always give the answer that I want, but I do believe that the company is serious about listening and considering it, and even if they say no this year they do say that I can come back the following year and reopen the conversation. It gives me hope.

In 2011, I did the company's first materiality matrix,[3] a process that looks at how external stakeholders' expectations of UPS dovetail or diverge from our executives' view of what sustainability efforts are tied to the company's business success. This process considered feedback from more than 100 outside groups, assessors and activist groups and will guide UPS's sustainability efforts for years to come. We are already at work on the next report, which I'm editing.

UPS has given me a great platform to learn about what other people are doing and about how to make change. I share those lessons today with MBA [Master of Business Administration] classes, sustainability leaders and others . . . because the best thing about sustainability is that we are all focused on making the world better.

Captain Chris Schroeder, Senior Manager Corporate Social Responsibility, Qatar Airways (Qatar)

I always knew I wanted to be a pilot. I discovered my love for flying when I was six – the freedom that flying offered, to get away from walls, machine guns and boundaries. I've seen how airplanes can bring food and services to a famine-struck area, how airlines are essential for creating cities where there once was nothing – the challenges that we can face and overcome, the adventures we can have, all because of the ability of flight. But this has to be in a positive way, in a way where what we create has positive, not negative, impacts. We help make that difference here at Qatar Airways.

I was brought up in West Berlin during the cold war, with the Wall around us and separated from the rest of Germany. A comfortable life, but still I was always aware of restricted freedom. In contrast to this, my British uncle was a pilot for Dan-Air and as a young boy he used to take me on his flights up and away from Berlin; the technical capacity of airplanes to create that freedom got me hooked. But being from

Berlin[4] I could not do German national service or join Lufthansa and so at the age of ten I faced my first challenge, got creative and wrote off to airlines and companies like Boeing, looking for opportunities to fly. In the end, with the help of my uncle, I joined the US Airforce and got a US flying licence, then a UK flying licence in Oxford when I was studying there. And then, just as I was ready to fly, the Maggie Thatcher effect hit the aviation industry.[5] She killed the aviation industry in the UK as airline after airline went bust.

And so I started flying for the United Nations (UN) in Africa, the Middle East and later in Vietnam. I did not know there were full-blown wars, famines and conflict. I was somewhat naive! There was nothing there, really nothing but refugee camps and real poverty. The flying was challenging, dangerous but important – delivering medical supplies, doctors and UN peacekeepers. I was really helping, adding personal value.

Eventually, due to corruption (which seemed prevalent in such UN-related activities), the flying service got shut down. But around this time my uncle, who was my mentor, died. He had been working for Singapore Airlines and I felt I owed it to him to join them. And so at the young age of 23 I was flying jumbo jets in Asia. Singapore was politically very interesting – at that time it was building itself up from a swamp. The airline was helping with that and aiming to be the world's best airline. It was good to be part of that, building a country and building an airline. But there were a lot of long-haul flights and when two and a half years later I got an opportunity to join Kuwait Airways, I jumped at the chance.

Kuwait was just coming out of war and devastation and needed to build itself up again. This was a blessing, to have this opportunity to be part of that. As a pilot I was part of the team that helped rebuild the airline, at times difficult, but we just got on with it – in a spirit of adventure! And I loved this, finding a way to overcome challenges. I only left there because the airline was nationalised and political will wanted Kuwaiti nationals as pilots. I was also starting to get bored though – the thrill of adventure was no longer so present.

So I joined Emirates, also building itself up at that time. I was with them for seven years, during which time I also studied for a couple of Masters and then set up a company advising airlines how to build themselves up, develop and expand their services. It was where I could be constructive and challenged. I got involved in change management within an airline in the Eastern Bloc, as this was when the USSR collapsed and Eastern European countries needed to build up their airlines, embrace new technology and change. So, for example, I helped with the privatisation of Slovak Airlines. I appreciate this was because of my unique experience, but still, these experiences sparked an intellectual interest in strategic change management. It also helped me realise that it's important to not forget where you come from, that your past will help shape where you are going.

I ran this consultancy for a decade and it was great to see the results of what we did. But it got to the point where flying for Emirates and running a consultancy was too much and I had to decide – flying or management. And that was a hard choice! But then an opportunity arose via Emirates with IATA [International Air Transport Association] (an airline membership group) to be Global Head of Flight Operations in Canada. I could combine flying with management. At IATA I saw that the environment was rising on the agenda and I could see this was an opportunity to do something meaningful and impactful about that. I took on and expanded the Fuel Efficiency Programme. Boeing started to push the agenda and in North America CSR [corporate social responsibility] (as it was called then) was becoming part of culture. I created best-practice sharing, green teams and processes to help improve technology. To me it made sense – the environmental concerns were real and significant. What we do now will have a lasting effect, so let's get it right. We introduced Lean 6 Sigma,[6] instigated proper change management processes and professionalised the agenda to get airlines to be fuel-efficient.

In 2007 Qatar Airways called in IATA for advice on fuel efficiency. We consulted for them and advised them of how they needed to change. The CEO [Chief Executive Officer] there is an unusual man, not afraid of action and very forward-thinking. He took our recommendations and then said to me: 'OK, great, thanks – so come on board and take us there. We have no one else that can do this but you.' Qatar at this time was very exciting – starting from very little and building itself up. I was missing the Middle East and I could see that with the commitment and support from the CEO of Qatar Airways I could create real change – have a real impact. When you look at what Qatar are doing – as a country they don't have a five-year plan but a 30-year plan. They were building, creating something, and I could be part of that again. I can see the results of what we do and what the country is doing, and that is a great motivation.

I do admire the approach and forward-looking mindset of our CEO (Akbar Al Baker) – and I have his support, and he is part of growing this country. Energy security is critical and even though current wealth is from oil, they know this is only temporary. Growth needs to happen but in a sustainable way; we need to find fuel alternatives. So I was given an open book to create a department to do this and I just got on with it. We look at fuel efficiency, alternative fuels and reducing environmental impact. But when we look at the issues at a country level, water is more critical. So we need sustainable development and as an airline not compete for scarce materials such as water. Such challenges are exciting and so important to overcome. And I feel we will in Qatar. The culture here is forward-thinking; the uniqueness of the society here is to be open-minded to new ideas with a real thirst for knowledge and advancement. And society is important to them, advancing health and education and wellbeing. All this is important to me, something I can be part of.

There are four other Specialists especially to recognise and thank for sharing their time, experiences and insight:

Dr Charlotte Grezo is Group Director of Corporate Responsibility Strategy at Centrica (UK). Charlotte has worked as a Specialist for over 15 years. She started her career as a Specialist after her PhD in Environmental Biology (her passion since she was 12). She talks about a determination to make a difference, create impact and be challenged. She says this has shaped the roles she has chosen and the work she does. Charlotte looks to be challenged and has chosen positions in BP, Vodafone, Lehman Brothers and now Centrica because she saw the opportunity to rise to a challenge, create change and make a positive difference. Charlotte's number-one recommendation for other Specialists is to have CEO support.

Angel Fraile has worked as Sustainable Development Manager at Endesa (Spain) for the last 6 years. Raised in a Catholic environment, Angel completed a degree in Law, Economics and Business Science and started working in corporate law. He then moved to Endesa for the opportunity to work for a large multinational. However, encouraged by the Argentinian film *A Place in the World*,[7] he realised he found his passion to make a difference and be challenged. Angel contacted the director in charge of sustainability to discuss his wider vision for Endesa and when the opportunity arose Angel joined them to help redefine uncertainty and professionalise their efforts. He feels he has found the place he wants to be, and has since taken a Master's Degree in Corporate Responsibility and a Postgraduate Degree in Corporate Reputation to further his knowledge. He now also teaches at several European business schools.

Andre Fourie is Head of Sustainable Development at the South African Breweries (SAB), the local subsidiary of SABMiller, the second largest brewer in the world. Andre was brought up in apartheid South Africa and the political climate before and after Nelson Mandela was released greatly influenced who he is today. As a child Andre remembers being shocked by the behaviour of his community because of what he saw in apartheid South Africa. He was committed to making a personal contribution to change, which was expressed in his role in the Consultative Business Movement (CBM), a group of business leaders committed to change the country's political economy. In this capacity he served as the CEO of the Business Election Fund, a business-based initiative to support a free and democratic election. After the first democratic elections in 1994, he joined the National Business Initiative (NBI), which was leading the efforts of business to help democracy work in the country. Andre worked his way up to be CEO of the NBI and personally championed environmental and social issues to the business community.[8] Recognising the power of business to get things done, in 2010 he moved to SAB, which is a leading player on the sustainability agenda in the South African corporate landscape.

Joe Franses is Director of Corporate Responsibility and Sustainability at Coca-Cola Enterprises. Joe grew up in the UK and throughout childhood and as a young adult he was an active member of a 'left of centre' youth movement, which helped to shape his values and politics. After university Joe worked as a consultant and was given the opportunity to work alongside Amanda Jordan, Geoffrey Bush and other founding-board members of the Corporate Responsibility Group, who introduced him to the field of corporate sustainability. Determined to make a career in this field, he joined Cable & Wireless as a Community Investment Manager and then moved to Coca-Cola Enterprises in 2005. He has worked there since then and feels he has found an organisation and role that fit well with who he is, and that has a culture and mission enabling him to make a difference on environmental and social issues. In 2011 Coca-Cola Enterprises published its own sustainability plan, *Deliver for Today, Inspire for Tomorrow*, which outlines a set of step-change sustainability commitments it aims to achieve by 2020 and sets them on a path towards being a low-carbon zero-waste business.

2.2 The corporate Sustainability Specialist

Being a Specialist is about having a real, tangible and positive impact. It is about dedicating your career to making a difference, to finding where societal and environmental need meets business benefit. It is about creating a business that can be a force for good with a net positive[9] footprint.

> This is a role that has impact; we shape problems beyond a normal sphere of influence.
>
> (Andre, SABMiller)

But make no mistake – being a Specialist is about making change and this can be difficult, sometimes unwelcomed, often initially alone, and a hard, long journey with a sometimes resistant or apathetic workforce. It is not an easy specialism to work in.

It can be tough. When you face resistance, you have to find a way to overcome – try, try and try again.

(Charlotte, Centrica)

The role of a corporate Sustainability Specialist is complex and challenging; the role typically takes a multidisciplinary approach as it is 'essential to have a wide range of issues knowledge, from CO2 footprint to social impact, legal issues' (Joe, Coca-Cola Enterprises). Table 2.1 reveals the range of tasks that the Sustainability Specialist of today typically undertakes.

Why is this profession emerging so quickly; and why now? Social movement theory (Fuchs, 2006) can help explain this. As described earlier, social movement theory looks at how society shifts from one phase of normality to the next. It explains that, when a number of society's members 'rebel' against their social norms, this can cascade into larger numbers that eventually transform society from one phase to the next – e.g. pre- to post-apartheid. Current discussion in academia postulates that we are living through such a social movement, from an unsustainable and resource-wasteful society to (hopefully) a sustainable one.[10] John Elkington (2012) is one such expert writing extensively on the need for a global shift in mindset, value and behaviours. He discusses the need to 'breach the sustainability chasm' in order to change society's values and behaviours.

Social movement typically starts with only a few of society's members challenging the dominant norms (Fuchs, 2006), such as Andre (SABMiller) growing up in apartheid South Africa (although there are other examples where being a member of a new social movement is less obvious or overt). The purpose is not individual gain; rather, the purpose is to create positive social change. Charlotte has a clear memory of a point in time in childhood when she realised she needed to be part of a new way of life, a new social norm. This has shaped her career choices:

I always remember that moment – it was clear as a bell. I was 12 and was watching fishes swim in a stream near my house and I knew, I just knew. I want to work on the relationship between man and the environment. It had to change, has to change. This is how I can help . . . I have never swayed from this, never doubted this.

(Charlotte, Centrica)

Sustainability Specialists are in theory at the vanguard of the sustainability social movement (Bendell, 2009), with a determination to build something new.

We had the freedom to develop a set of sustainability commitments representing a new mindset of how we do business . . . within this, I had the ability to develop, explore and challenge things.

(Joe, Coca-Cola Enterprises)

Table 2.1 Typical tasks a Sustainability Specialist undertakes

Team management	Manage a team of direct reports and indirect reports Manage consultants
Stakeholder management	Engage with key stakeholders, such as customer groups, NGOs, government bodies, community groups Develop strategic partnerships with industry and key NGOs and be responsible for those relationships Network and build advocates – inside and outside the business Stakeholder mapping, engagement and management, including setting up and running stakeholder panels and committees
Programme management	Develop, plan and supervise initiative/project development, including community investment, and initiatives run with partners such as United Nations Global Compact, certification bodies and charities/NGOs Monitor and audit the success of these activities, and feed back into business and stakeholders for continued development
Change management	Set up and run organisation-wide change management programmes with other departments, with a focus on behaviour change Engage employees and key stakeholders in the change programmes Work with other department leads one on one to embed new codes, processes and intellectual capital into existing systems, such as Human Resources, Finance, Facilities, Production
Influencing and networking	Develop internal employee champion network, to help employees take ownership of change Develop external learning networks with key stakeholders and new stakeholders (i.e. industry experts, academics) to help engage, learn and influence
Management systems	Introduce auditing, ranking and indices submissions Advise on operational policies, procedures, systems and programmes Advise and/or lead on setting up management systems such as ISO, certification and reporting systems needed for reporting for GRI, SRI or integrated reporting Help to set up environmental management systems to report and set targets for climate change, energy, waste and water use Create codes of conduct and internal standards Manage budgets and work with Finance on some finance management and reporting systems
Employee communication and education	Run internal marketing and communications programmes Set up and run in-house training programmes

Table 2.1 Continued

Strategic input	Develop a sustainability strategy and create a framework and set of tactics
	Develop goals, measurements and key performance indicators for department and advise at company level
	Report to and advise Board members twice a year
	Liaise with NED/Director as direct report on progress and advise on action needed by leaders of the organisation
	Build the business case for specific programmes, with defined ROI
	Internal consultancy, whether cultural issues, legal standards, business ethics
Reporting and communications	Create/help create frameworks for measurements, collecting data, reporting frameworks and disseminating
	Work with the Finance and Communications team on sustainability reporting
	Submit to indices and track progress
	Coordinate validation, auditing and certification of reporting
Represent the organisation externally	Advocacy on specific issues
	Presentations at conferences, board meetings and investor relation events

Compiled from an analysis of job descriptions and adverts, literature review and case study analysis from 2006 to 2012.

NGOs, non-governmental organisations; ISO, International Organization for Standardization; GRI, Global Reporting Initiative; SRI, socially responsible investment; NED, non-executive director; ROI, return on investment.

2.3 Understanding the Specialist

A clear observation from the research was the consistency of three specific linear moments in the lives of the Specialists interviewed, which created:

1. A *seed* (event or influence) in their early history that connects with their chosen career. For example, Lynnette's (UPS) seed is growing up in the politically turbulent '60s and '70s with socially active parents and being personally exposed to social change. This helped to develop her desires as a Specialist to understand the bigger picture, help create positive social change and take on challenging issues.
2. An *awakening* moment, where this seed was given the opportunity to grow. For example, Chris's (Qatar Airways) experiences flying for the UN awakened him to international development and country building.
3. The moment of *opportunity*. Both Lynnette and Chris have had more than one opportunity – but the first time they were able to align their awakened 'seed' closely with their job is a crystal-clear memory for both. For example, Lynnette seeing the opportunity for how her clients could help the slum children in Bangkok.

The stories of Lynnette (UPS) and Chris (Qatar Airways) are honest personal reflections of how childhood experiences shaped how (and why) they undertake their jobs and how they conduct themselves as Specialists today. Revealing such early learned experiences[11] and upbringing helps understand how and why the development of this new profession is being shaped by those working in it as much as it is being shaped by what business requires of the profession.

2.3.1 A sense of self

Without delving deeply into Freudian theory of ego, it is worth looking at the strong 'sense of self' that our Specialists have (Freud *et al.*, 2009). People develop different degrees of clarity and appreciation of who they are as individuals and in the wider world – the clarity they have of values, characteristics and cognitive reasoning, and the unique identity that each of us has in the world ('meaning of life'). As described earlier, some scientists, such as Viktor Frankl, postulate that finding sources of meaning of life (such as a job) can reinforce our sense of self (Frankl, 1964). I propose that Specialists have a high need to seek such meaning-driven roles because of, and also to reinforce, their strong sense of self and desire to define the 'meaning of their life', or their unique contribution in the world (Visser, 2008). Thus, when they find such a position, the role itself can seem like '*this* is where I belong' (Angel, Endesa).

Specialists seem to have very clear and fixed self-identity.[12] Angel (Endesa) has a clear understanding of his 'self' and is not willing to compromise on this:

> I have a set of values that I do not compromise on. I won't compromise who I am to succeed.
>
> (Angel, Endesa)

Angel knows of examples in previous positions when his fixed self-identity and unwillingness to take action contrary to that hindered his career progression – but still he refuses to compromise. Many employees will experience moments when they face the choice of taking opportunistic action that conflicts with their belief of what is right or wrong – but for Specialists this strong sense of self guides them past those options. I argue that this sense of self originates in childhood and helps Specialists have a clear self-identity as an adult, influencing in a very specific way what their responses are to issues they face at work (Bansal, 2003).

> My uncle always reinforced the importance of a positive mindset. Take a challenge and be creative . . . this is who I am today.
>
> (Chris, Qatar Airways)

Some of the Specialists also spoke of experiences in childhood when the values that made up their sense of self were challenged. For them the realisation that the social norms of the collective around them did not include these values was a shock. Andre shares his personal experience of this:

> I was brought up in white South Africa, with church values and a respect for authority and the system. When I realised what it was like for the black person outside my world – it shook me to the core. I instantly knew this was wrong, not what I had been taught. I was disillusioned and did not see the value in being part of that society.
>
> (Andre, SABMiller)

It was only when the social norm around him adjusted – or he found a new 'collective'[13] that reflected and reinforced his sense of self – that he felt more connected with his surroundings. A sense of belonging, passion for his work and success followed. It could be that this experience helped to strengthen that determination not to compromise on his sense of self in adulthood.

> When Nelson Mandela was freed . . . it was a huge release, a wild moment for me. This was something I could be part of.
>
> (Andre, SABMiller)

For employees generally, the workplace can often be the 'collective' that reinforces the sense of self and enables them to flourish. For Specialists, who already have a strong and fixed sense of self, finding the right collective can create employees that are highly trustworthy and reliable. It is perhaps no coincidence that all those interviewed are well respected and have earned the trust and counsel of the senior actors in their organisation. This is remarkable considering that the nature of their job is to challenge the status quo, uncover the uncomfortable truths and change the norm of the organisation.

Whether they are representatives of a new social movement attempting to change us from an unsustainable to sustainable society (as Angel of Endesa says, 'inside the revolution') – or simply some of society's outliers with very strong self-identity and determination to build something new – their sense of self has shaped who they are as Specialists and the companies they choose to work with, and has contributed to why they are successful.

2.4 Advice for Specialists

Recognising the unique role and characteristics of a Specialist predicates the advice that this role is one suited to only a small group of individuals. However, for those who recognise themselves in the shared stories, or are struggling Specialists, the following advice may help.

2.4.1 Recognise your motivation

The functional role of Specialists is actively to make changes (Table 2.1). Conversely, the research clearly shows that Specialists as individuals have a need to create, and see the results of, impact and change.

> You start to say, okay what difference can I personally make and then what difference can I make using the resources of the clients or the employers that I have to make a difference. And what we do actually does make a difference.
>
> (Lynnette, UPS)

One can speculate what came first – the need for an organisational sustainability change-maker or the Specialist's need for a job that creates change. However, it is clear that the ability to create impact is the significant motivator for Specialists taking on difficult tasks – to the extent that not being able to have real impact can indicate a misfit between the individual and the company:

> I would join a bad company if I could make a difference; I would leave a good one if I could not.
>
> (Andre, SABMiller)

Visiting the operations of the business and partners, suppliers, and where initiatives are being run – not just for operational reasons but also to connect with the people there and hear what changes they are going through – can help weary Specialists remember the impact they are having. Seeing the change being made to real lives is a powerful motivator, a way to 'recharge the batteries' (Joe, Coca-Cola Enterprises).

It also helps to be clear and articulate how you are contributing. Likewise, being clear how the sustainability team and the organisation is having a positive impact also helps; for example, by connecting individual tasks – which can sometimes get lost in the bigger picture – to the overall corporate strategy, with defined markers for how different activities support that strategy. This helps not just Specialists and their team, but also other employees who can then understand why Specialists do what they do.

2.4.2 Feed your intellectual curiosity

Specialists seem to have an almost insatiable appetite for learning, challenging and pushing themselves, coupled with a desire to 'understand what is going on in the world' (Charlotte, Centrica).

> I love a challenge, needing to find a way through.
>
> (Andre, SABMiller)

> I enjoy being challenged, pushed.
>
> (Joe, Coca-Cola Enterprises)

For a Specialist, choosing an organisation to work for relies not only on the direct team and organisation and its reputation, but also on the industry. The words 'dynamic', 'fast-pace' and 'innovative' were consistently used to describe the industry, company and team members the Specialists work with. Being part of not just an organisation, but also a wider movement that is challenging the status quo and working at a fast pace is a significant attraction for Specialists. Chris (Qatar Airways) describes his attraction to working in the Middle East where the environment is dynamic, challenging and fast-pace, and to taking on ever-more challenging roles. Lynnette (UPS) talks about her attraction to logistics and supply chain management as a dynamic and fast-moving industry.

Having significant curiosity about their external environment and an understanding of their connection to the 'bigger picture' drives our Specialists to 'horizon scan'[14] and stay up to date with the wider issues in the industry, environment, politics and emerging technology. This resonates with what organisations are asking Specialists to do (Table 2.1).

If you have intellectual curiosity and enjoy being challenged, invest some time in due diligence not only on the organisation, but also on the industry and direct team you would be working with. Recognise that you are curious and join relevant associations that expose you to wider issues (socio/economic/political/technical), find platforms for conversations and allow time in the job role for research and reading. Attend relevant conferences, read relevant literature and allow time to nurture your curiosity.

2.4.3 The importance of values or characteristics congruence

Many employees seek a degree of values congruence (Amos and Weathington, 2008) between their own values and those of the organisation they work for. This is both to feel a connection to a place they invest many hours in and also because becoming a member of a collective (collection of individuals, such as an organisation) helps to reinforce our own self-identity. For Specialists it is especially important to have a good degree of congruence, where their work reinforces their sense of self and uniqueness.

> My identity is tied into my work, into what I do at work. It is a good cultural fit.
>
> (Joe, Coca-Cola Enterprises)

Values congruence relates specifically to a match between personal values and the espoused values of an organisation – however, congruence can also relate to *characteristics* such as 'dynamic', 'forward-thinking', 'fast-pace' (in comparison to values of 'integrity' or 'respect'). This does not mean total congruence of every value and characteristic, but congruence to a degree that one feels comfortable with. Andre (SABMiller), for example, talks of his willingness to join a 'bad' organisation (performing badly in a sustainable sense) *as long as* that organisation is ready and willing to change. Without doubt the true values of an organisation are critical, but if a 'bad' organisation has a genuine desire to change then this sends signals of other appealing characteristics such as needing their expertise, and having a leader challenging the status quo. Charlotte (Centrica) talks about the characteristics of BP she was attracted to outside what BP actually does:

> I was stimulated by the people, they were a fascinating company. At the time they had a great reputation for being dynamic, and were creating new processes, a CEO who wanted to change.
>
> (Charlotte Grezzo, on BP)

Experienced Specialists will probably be aware of reputations and actions of organisations they are looking to join. If not, due diligence, such as a review of articles, annual reports, awards, case studies and third-party analysis can help give a more accurate understanding of the values of the organisation. However, look also for the characteristics of the organisation as there may be congruence with *how* the organisation works. Assessing what the leaders of the organisation say is a good tactic in understanding if there is characteristics congruence. CEO reports, letters to shareholders, opening letters on annual report, speeches and articles from board members can give insight into what is truly 'on the corporate agenda'. Sometimes an organisation may recruit for a sustainability team where no board members or C-suite support[15] is available; this can reflect lack of senior support and buy-in and display negative characteristics. Active CEO support is essential and also reflects the values and characteristics of the organisation.

> I insist on meeting the CEO before I accept a role. Without the CEO's support real change won't happen, and it is time to move on.
>
> (Charlotte, Centrica)

2.4.4 Beware!

The role can be a lonely one, and frustrating – especially as Specialists are change-makers and can be seen as disruptive.

> We can be seen as an outsider, asking the uncomfortable questions. But when outside the firm we are seen as a company person.
>
> (Angel, Endesa)

It helps to build allies, and earning trust from fellow employees and organisational leaders is critical. Many Specialists join professional associations, such as the Corporate Responsibility Officers Association, International Society of Sustainability Practitioners, Association of Sustainability Professionals and Global Association of Corporate Sustainability Officers, and country-specific organisations where they can share best practice and explore relevant issues. Finding a mentor, or Godparent, in the organisation can also significantly help, as explored further in Chapter 5. However, the essential personal competency is strength – or, as Charlotte (Centrica) says, 'Be robust, self-sufficient and confident.'

Further, many Specialists report that their teams tend to be too small for the amount of work they have to do. This is sometimes linked to budget, but other times to the structure of an organisation (i.e. matrix or hierarchical), or that the business case for a fully equipped team is not yet proved. Creating a 'Champions' network' (see Chapter 4) can help, as can clearly defining and articulating the business case to key decision-makers.

Not having support or buy-in from employees – or not having the time to build this up – is also problematic but can be overcome. This can sometimes manifest as organisational inertia or employee lack of interest. If the organisation is only starting to explore what being a responsible organisation means, if there is lack of staff knowledge of sustainability and the team, or if 'CSR' previously meant community projects or philanthropy, then sustainability needs to be proven as core to organisational success. These barriers can be overcome with education, communication and engagement tactics. However, if there are deeper issues in the culture of the organisation which discourage change or learning, employee engagement or even cross-business communication, these are cultural issues that can be significant barriers (see Chapter 1 for more discussion on culture).

2.5 Advice for organisations

Corporate Sustainability Specialists are valuable additions to any organisation. Organisations can no longer ignore the societal, economic and environmental stresses that exist. Being sustainable refers to our ability to ensure that what we do today to survive into tomorrow will cause no harm to future generations surviving into their tomorrows. When thinking logically about that, what business would admit to taking action today that knowingly harms its ability to survive in the future? This is the fundamental role of Specialists – helping their organisations to achieve this seemingly logical, but still difficult, task. However, a few leading organisations and best-practice Specialists take this a step further and recognise that organisations must be a positive force in the world:

> At the start of 2012 we announced a new corporate responsibility plan called 'Kingfisher Net Positive'. It commits us to a new challenge: to go beyond neutrality, to no longer strive to 'do less' but to seek to make a positive contribution to the world's future. Zero isn't enough, neutral

isn't enough. Better means doing more good, not just less bad. So the challenge we have set ourselves is to have a *net positive impact*. Our business will put back more than it takes out . . . and we are putting a demanding strategy behind it.

(Ian Cheshire, Chief Executive Kingfisher Group, 2012[16])

If further argument is needed for the role of the Specialist, there are proven business benefits which are summarised in a 2011 Business in the Community (BITC) and Doughty Centre Centre for Corporate Responsibility report. For a leading retailer's perspective see the UK retailer M&S 2012 report on its business benefits.

2.5.1 Recruiting a Specialist

The average Specialist can be highly qualified, with at least a first degree and probably a second, more specialist degree (MBA or MSc), usually focused in a relevant area (e.g. environment, community, finance or economics). Some have a specific postgraduate Masters degree in corporate responsibility and a few have PhDs.

Experience tends to be mainly from a different business discipline from inside or outside the organisation (whether same industry sector, consultancy or third sector) (Acre, Ancona, 2012). For example, a 2010 US survey revealed that over 95% came from other backgrounds, such as finance, marketing or logistics (Boston College Center for Corporate Citizenship – BCCCC, 2010). Their experience was relevant to the focus that their sustainability job tended to have – for example, social sustainability, such as ethical trading/bribery/human rights law experience from working in supplier management; environmental sustainability focus from experience of energy efficiency projects, or implementing ISO standards.

Titles range from Directors or Heads of Department, Managers, Advisors to Assistants. However, across the business, the roles tend to be middle- to senior-level positions in the organisation, from Manager upwards. In Asia, it is interesting to note that the corporate sustainability teams tend to be very small groups or an individual but that 71% were senior managers or operating at board level (CSR Asia, 2008).

In 2012 the level of seniority of the professional was reflected in pay scales, earning £40,000–£60,000 per annum for middle-level positions and £60,000–£80,000 for senior Specialists – although for those in FTSE100 companies the earning tendency was £80,000–£100,000 per annum, with Director or Head of Sustainability earning over £85,000 and the most junior individuals (assistants) earning £20,000–£25,000.

Reporting tends to be directly to the senior officers of the organisation – whether Head of Department/Director or directly to the CEO or CFO. Encouragingly, 2012 data from the FTSE100[17] show that at least 89% of companies have a board member with direct and specific responsibility for sustainability and 97% have a specific structure in place in the organisation to house the sustainability professionals (i.e. a department or formal structured network).

For this profession, the gender split is currently more even than seen in more traditional business professions – slightly more females than males· Conflicting data suggests more females year on year are entering the profession compared with a 2012 study that showed more men were entering the profession. However, as with most professions (business or public sector), the more senior positions tend to be held by men and on average men are earning more than women.[18]

2.5.2 Competencies and skills of a Specialist

What can organisations do to enable Specialists in their role? Firstly, understand the skills and competencies a Specialist needs, which can help in recruitment, identification and training. Table 2.2 summarises these, compiled from interviews, literature review and scanning job adverts. This is a 'wish list' as it is comprehensive and calls for a very senior and highly competent individual, and so can also be seen as a guide for longer-term training and development of Specialists.

2.5.3 Budgets

Budgets can be a particular problem – whether a limited team budget or where budgets are held by other departments and the Specialists negotiate or bargain for resource. Some Specialists (and those who manage Specialists) advise that a minimum budget is essential for the team, not only as a staffing resource but also to send a strong signal of investment for the work the team does. An inadequate budget requires the team constantly to build a business case for every project or activity being resourced from elsewhere in the business – or, more frustratingly, continuously to have to justify their very existence in the organisation.

It helps if the CEO and CFO recognise that sustainability is a long-term investment (not a cost) and whereas it is good practice to budget, forecast and assess suitability of activities, sometimes 'leaps of faith' need to be made. A discussion, framed around building the business case for sustainability, could help CEOs or CFOs understand how sustainable business can be an investment rather than a cost. Traditional measurements (such as standard internal rate of return or net present value[19]) can be incompatible with the return seen from being a sustainable business (both in time period and type of return, as often the financial return generated is in other departments, such as cost reduction in facilities or logistics/transport). However, metrics have improved dramatically over the last decade and are now available to track improvements in innovation generation, employee engagement, cost mini-misation and risk management.[20] Some companies will set aside a budget

Table 2.2 Competencies and skills of a Specialist

Competencies	
Thought leadership	Communication skills
Selling and persuading	Creative problem solving
Strategic vision	Horizon scanning/seeing the bigger picture
Leading people and setting a good example	Being credible and having gravitas
Being approachable	A good networker
Understanding the politics of an organisation	Well informed and trend spotting
Being resilient	Innovative thinking and able to seek out innovative thinking and technologies
Strong business basics	Commercial acumen, including from profit and loss exposure
Influencing ability	Being flexible
Expert knowledge	Results-oriented

Skills	
Ability to analyse and understand data	Understanding motivations for behaviour and how to change that (including engagement)
Running change programmes	Developing identity and helping employees develop understanding
Facilitating meetings, workshops and meetings with external parties	Developing strategies
Building a business case	Creating a tactical plan, and measuring and reporting on progress
Stakeholder engagement and management	Writing skills
Running training and education programmes	Interpreting and translating
Presentation skills	Running internal cross-functional working groups or projects
Learning on the job	Tri-sector partnering experience
Getting on agendas and agenda setting	Experience across several functions and markets
Finding business opportunities	Engaging with senior leaders and/or board members
Technical experience addressing sustainability issues, from human rights to CO_2 emissions, diversity to ethical trade	Ability to switch from acting independently to working within a team

for 'experimentation', for example projects the sustainability team think will be beneficial but do not yet have a clear business case for. Leading UK retailers Marks & Spencer (see Chapter 1) have an Innovation Fund to test projects and prove to other departments they are worth investing in.

2.5.4 Motivating Specialists

Useful insight for the Human Resources team and those managing Specialists is that Specialists (perhaps more than other employees) tend to link to a high degree their own personal identity with that of the organisation and what they are doing in their role. The psychological contract they have with the organisation is highly personal, and can therefore be very strong – but if broken it can be highly disruptive.

> Not that I can see this happening at Coca-Cola Enterprises, but if I believed that an organisation I work for ever caused harm on purpose – not because of a mistake, but on purpose – that would be deeply frustrating and challenge my commitment to the organisation.
>
> (Joe, Coca-Cola Enterprises)

Thus, work motivation can be different to that of the average middle manager; although Sustainability professionals can be well qualified and experienced and therefore can command good salaries, surveys have shown that the top two motivations for what Specialists do is for the challenge (to have a role exploring new frontiers), and to make a positive impact on business and society (to make a positive difference) (Boston College Center for Corporate Citizenship – BCCCC, 2010). The Specialists profiled in this chapter did not go into this field for career advancement (although seniority is essential to enable real change) – rather for a mission, with rewards beyond solely financial rewards. It is critical to recognise this in how they are recruited, retained, rewarded and motivated.

As explored earlier, it is important to acknowledge that positive values/ characteristics and the ability to make an impact are critical in motivating and getting the best from Specialists. Setting challenges and stretching but achievable targets, and being given public recognition of the importance of the work they do, by the CEO, for example, can motivate them more than a financial bonus. Specialists could also get bored more quickly than the average employee, but helping them to see the difference they make could compensate for this (i.e. rewards such as visits to community outreach programmes to see work taking place).

2.5.5 Power and authority

For those directly managing or overseeing Specialists – whether directors or board members – it is useful to know that not having leadership support is a significant problem, especially if the leader is absent or, worse, unsupportive.

Top leadership support (C-suite, board director) is essential. That leader must not just espouse support, but actively lead – talk about what the business is doing, highlight success stories in press interviews, speak at conferences, comment on the annual and sustainability reports, create access for the Specialists to people across the business, update shareholders on sustainability performance, engage senior people in the business and publicly support the work the Specialists and Champions do.

It is important for those managing Specialists to give the necessary power, or authority, to Specialists to enable them in their work. There are three types of relevant power available to give, in varying degrees dependent on the culture of the organisation and nature of the people involved:

1. *Borrowed*: power inherent in the system and processes such as rank, which can be lent to a Specialist for a period of time (Balogun *et al.*, 2005). Further, if the organisational leader sanctions 'insurgency' (i.e. change) then authority can be 'lent' to the change-maker to carry out that change.[21] This is in part why it is so important to have active CEO support. Godparents often 'lend' power (explored in Chapter 5):

    > It is essential to have the moral authority to do the work. The CEO or leader of the firm can give this to me and I can earn it personally.
    > (Angel, Endesa)

2. *Earned authority*: the Specialist may not have positional power but because of good past performance and relationships the person is respected and listened to and therefore has earned moral authority (Lawrence *et al.*, 2006).

3. *Positional power*: the Specialist has a senior position embedded within the system, with resources such as budget and an authentic and powerful reporting line, such as a director or C-suite role (Balogun *et al.*, 2005).

    > I've earned my bosses' trust because I'm good at my job. Status and where you sit is also very important.
    > (Charlotte, Centrica)

A fourth type of power – *entrepreneurial* power, gained from unsanctioned bureaucratic insurgency – is when managers take power without permission in order to carry out their job.[22] This can be disruptive (in a negative or positive way) and lending or giving change-makers some power to do things can be more constructive and preferable, especially when the power is clearly directed to the corporate agenda (Zald, 2005).

In summary, the strongest enabler an organisation can put in place is for the CEO actively to support and advocate the work that Specialists do.

2.5.6 The power of space

> I have great trust from my boss and have the freedom and space to just
> get on with it.
>
> (Chris, Qatar Airways)

Because the profession of the corporate Sustainability Specialist is relatively
new, experimentation is still in progress. Job roles often evolve quite fast as
organisations quickly recognise the wider spectrum of issues and impacts
material to them. This can be exciting and rewarding for organisations as
they find benefits not predicted – such as when exploring new forms of
relationships with suppliers or other industry members (such as business-led
coalitions, supplier networks or cross-industry issue-specific alliances) that
result in new and better products, less risky supply chains with more
sustainable raw materials, cost savings and efficiency in operations (BITC
and Doughty Centre, 2011). However, it can also be unpredictable and
introduce a need for new skills such as stakeholder management and being
able to balance transparency with risk from sharing sensitive propriety
information with external stakeholders (BITC, 2012).

Specialists, and, indeed, employees across the business need to learn these
new skills.

> We are living increasingly in a world that is more volatile . . . I describe
> the world using the acronym, VUCA: volatile, uncertain, complex and
> ambiguous. Close your eyes and try to walk around – it's a very uncom-
> fortable feeling. Blind people, actually, are ideal people to learn from
> because they experience many situations as uncertain and complex. And
> many of the skills they use to cope with those situations are exactly the
> skills that managers now need to run their businesses.
>
> (Paul Poleman, CEO Unilever: PWC, 2011)

Learning these skills requires tools to experiment and learn, such as: access
to the latest research and development, time to explore the wider societal/
economic/environmental trends, access to academic and sustainability
thinking, and skills for horizon scanning. Specifically for Specialists, this
requires permission to take risks and explore meaning. They can be more
successful if given 'managerial discretion'[23] to explore the variables and
consider action based on a multiple of factors (not just financial). For example,
discretion or 'space' for reflection and experimentation could be explicitly
written into job descriptions. Sometimes, the scope of roles and responsibilities
is too narrow (e.g. including only looking at environmental impacts of the
organisation) and so a process needs to be in place to allow Specialists to raise
issues that may not have been identified within that scope or are not currently
on the corporate agenda. A clear corporate strategic agenda (and sending
the correct signals of what is on that agenda – Bansal, 2003) is therefore

critical, but mechanisms that allow the agenda to be discussed are also advantageous for the organisation.

> I question things a lot. I think over time this has been my greatest value to UPS – and they listen to me . . . They don't always give the answer that I want, but I do believe that the company is serious about listening and considering it, and even if they say no this year they do say that I can come back the following year and reopen the conversation.
>
> (Lynnette, UPS)

2.6 Concluding thoughts

In 2011 a report from the Global Association of Corporate Sustainability Officers (GACSO) called for better codification of the Sustainability Specialist profession:

> There is currently little consensus about what the sustainability role involves and what makes a good corporate sustainability professional. The lack of a clearly defined skill set prevents effective recruitment and frustrates the development of compelling career paths in this field.
>
> (GACSO, 2011)

This is typical for a new profession and in management education a selection of courses and certificates are now available – from a dedicated MBA at the University of Exeter in the UK (One Planet MBA), MSc in CSR/sustainability from leading business schools worldwide, to short courses run by associations such as Business in the Community in the UK, CSR Europe/Asia and Business for Social Responsibility, based in the USA. At the same time there is a global desire for some of the skill and mindset of a Sustainability Specialist to be reflected in all business education, so that all educated business professionals are thinking and acting in a sustainable way. The UN established an initiative to encourage this – to embed sustainability research and teaching into mainstream postgraduate business education. Called Principles of Responsible Management Education (PRME), in 2012 over 420 signatories globally had signed up to a set of principles to do just that. Slowly the education and qualifications, networks and associations, and unique skill and mindset of the Specialist are being appreciated and defined. The specialism is set for further change over the next decade, as it becomes more established, codified, appreciated and – as seen in this chapter – as it is shaped by those unique individuals working in the field.

2.6.1 Summary advice

- The role of the Sustainability Specialist is a new but emerging profession – it should be taken seriously as a critical business role, ensuring future success.

- Good Specialists are competent and qualified business people with a broad experience and skills across different sectors and industries, sometimes with both in-house and consultancy experience.
- The role of a Specialist has to be specific to the company's context and need, but there are a range of basic responsibilities that all Sustainability Specialists have and need.
- It is important that the company's leadership sends clear signals of what is on the corporate agenda. However, it is advantageous if the Specialist has access and permission to raise issues and questions not on the corporate agenda, if the Specialist builds a good business case for it.
- A clear set of organisational values not just helps to attract Specialists, but helps them to see what changes and initiatives are relevant to the mission and purpose of the organisation.
- Most Specialists invest themselves in the role and company, looking for a degree of values, characteristics or agenda congruence. The personal connection is important.
- It will greatly help a Specialist team do their job well if they have support from the leader, a degree of power or authority, a good degree of discretion in their role, resources and permission to learn and explore, and opportunities to make and see impact.
- The role of the Specialist can currently be tough and occasionally lonely. Attending conferences and workshops can help with personal development. Further, joining relevant Specialist networks can also help make connections.

2.7 Further reading

Acre (2011). *The Emergence of the Chief Sustainability Officer.* Business Report. .

Ashridge and Danish Commerce and Companies Agency (2005). *Catalogue of CSR Activities: A Broad Overview.* Online at: www.ashridge.org.uk/website/IC.nsf/wFARATT/Catalogue%20of%20CSR%20Activities:%20A%20broad%20overview/$file/CSRActivities.pdf (accessed March 2013).

Australian Centre for CSR (2007). *The CSR Manager in Australia: A Research Report.* Online at: www.accsr.com.au/pdf/ACCSR_Research_Report_CSR_Managers.pdf.

Boston College Center for Corporate Citizenship (2011). *Profile of the Profession.* Online at: www.bccorporatecitizenship.org

Collier J, Esteban R (2007). Corporate social responsibility and employee commitment. *Business Ethics: A European Review* 16 (1): 19–33.

Crane H, Kreula S (2006). *Working in CSR: What's it Really Like?* Online at: www.nottingham.ac.uk/shared/shared_careers/pdf/e-book_Working_in_CSR.pdf (accessed March 2013).

CROA (2011). *Structuring and Staffing Corporate Responsibility.* Corporate Responsibility Officer Association. Online at: www.croassociation.org.

CROA and Business Civic Leadership Center (2012). *The State of the Corporate Responsibility Profession.* Online at: www.croassociation.org.

CSR Asia (2008). *CSR in Asia: Who is Getting it Done?* Asia. Online at: http://www.csr-asia.com/report/report_csr_in_asia.pdf.

Doughty Centre for Corporate Responsibility and Odgers Berndston (2009). *Who Should Head Up your Corporate Responsibility Approach?* Cranfield: Cranfield School of Management. Online at: www.som.cranfield.ac.uk/som/p16340/Research/Research-Centres/Doughty-Centre-Home/Knowledge-Creation/Library-of-work/Document-Library.

Ferguson D (2010). *Measuring Business Value and Sustainability Performance.* Doughty Centre for Corporate Responsibility Occasional Paper. Online at: www.som.cranfield.ac.uk/som/dinamic-content/media/EABIS%20paper%20final.doc.pdf.

Gribben C (2007). *A Snapshot of Executive Development for Corporate Responsibility Professionals in the UK.* Ashridge: Ashridge Business School & CRG.

Kobayashi E, Kerbo HR, Sharp SF (2010). Differences in individual and collective tendencies among college students in Japan and US. *International Journal of Comparative Sociology* 51(1–2): 59–84.

Net Impact and Center for Corporate Citizenship at Boston College (2011). *Corporate Careers that Make a Difference.* Available for members or purchase only.

OSI (2008). Office of Science and Innovation definition, UK, from DSTL, Department of Defence. UK presentation.

PWC (2012). *Sustainability Valuation: An Oxymoron?* Online at: www.pwc.com/en_US/us/transaction-services/publications/assets/pwc-sustainability-valuation.pdf.

Reker GT, Wong PTP (1988). Aging as an individual process: Toward a theory of personal meaning. In JE Birren & VL Bengston (Eds.) *Emergent Theories of Aging* (pp. 214–246). New York, NY: Springer.

Reker GT, Peacock EJ, Wong PT (1987) Meaning and purpose in life and well-being: A life span perspective. *Journal of Gerontology* 42: 44–49.

Song MK (2009). The integrative structure of employee commitment. *Leadership and Organisational Development* 30 (3): 240–255.

Sustainability at Work (2012). *The Role, the Challenges, the Future: A First Look into the Sustainability Discipline.* Online at: www.sustainabilityatwork.com.au.

Visser W (2006). CSR managers as champions of change. ICCA CSR Briefing note.

Weinreb Group (2011). *CSO Back Story: How Chief Sustainability Officers Reached the c-Suite.* Online at: www.weinrebgroup.com.

3   The Social Intrapreneur

Social Intrapreneur: (noun) A person within a large corporation who takes direct action for innovation(s) which address social or environmental challenges profitably.

Social Intrapreneurs are a new type of employee that has emerged, notably over the last decade. Research is still ongoing about them but what is clear is the focused determination and drive they have to make significant change through the utilisation of organisational resources and capacity that exist in the businesses they are employed by. Social Intrapreneurs are entrepreneurial within organisations (hence *intra*preneurs).

We know that the number of social enterprises being created globally is on the increase, by social *entre*preneurs determined to find where social or environmental need meets business benefit and run this as a business. Many of these social entrepreneurs have left organisations because they could not do this from within organisations that did not share or support their vision – they could not be social *intra*preneurs within that organisation. As you will see from the case studies, this can often be a significant missed opportunity for business and potentially for the individual concerned too.

Social Intrapreneurs take direct action and challenge the organisation's status quo, perhaps more-so than Specialists and Champions. Social Intrapreneurs are able to develop scalable solutions to global challenges precisely because they are placed within organisations, able to utilise significant resources and therefore have significant impact. They can leverage existing infrastructure and organisational capacity to deliver social value on a large scale. They further a social or environmental goal whilst generating profit for their employees.

This chapter is based on emerging findings from a long-term research programme by the Doughty Centre for Corporate Responsibility, Cranfield School of Management. The team have identified a group of Social Intrapreneurs from across different business sectors around the world, and a book is in progress for 2013 publication. The stories of two of those Social Intrapreneurs are told here in depth but the chapter is based on an analysis of more, and summaries of those other stories will be available to read in 2013–14.[1] I would especially like to mention three Social Intrapreneurs additional to the two profiled here, for their detailed sharing and insight with the research team: Chris Harrop (Marshalls Plc, UK), Dorje Mundle (Novartis, Switzerland) and Emma Clarke (Babcock, UK).

3.1 Case studies

Sumanta Kumar De, General Manager, Olam (Indonesia)

I am entrepreneurial, I love building and creating. I like being close to the problem and searching for a solution. A sustainable business model is not about charity, it's about win–win solutions.

I was born in Jamshedpur, India, a large town that developed around a steel company (Tata Steel) in one of India's poorest states, Jharkhand. I had a relatively comfortable, middle-class childhood but did see lots of people well below the poverty line and really struggling – many were farmers who had given up on their farms and moved into the city to take on menial, low-paid work and were now worse off than before. The moment I would step out of city limits I could see poverty and extremely poor infrastructure; the town was an example of a well-developed oasis surrounded by undeveloped desert. At school I saw all types of classmates, from those really poor to the children of professors and managers working in the steel factory.

When I look back at my childhood I do think I was lucky due to the influence I had from both my parents and schooling. My parents focused on the values system, education and performance – integrity and honesty was always chosen over financial profit alone. I went to Jesuit schools and now realise that unconsciously some of these principles of simplicity, hard work and fairness have influenced my values in the long term. Luckily, I was a good student, won lots of scholarships and enjoyed learning.

I did a Bachelors Degree in Science at one of the best universities in India and then decided to do a postgraduate qualification in Industrial Relations and Labour Laws. I know it was not a typical decision; I did have offers to do finance/marketing and more traditionally lucrative subjects but I decided to follow my heart. People management really fascinates me, with a mix of both soft and hard skills. My education strengthened my belief that if you can get the people of an organisation engaged then, with people as key drivers, 70% of the job is done.

The places to work in India after a postgraduate degree are the blue-chip FMCG [fast-moving consumer goods] companies such as Unilever, Coca-Cola, Procter & Gamble or the banking industry. It was what was expected and so I went to work for Coca-Cola as a HR [human resources] professional. However, I quickly moved to the commercial part of the business. Well, what happened was that I had a mentor during my management training and he noticed my high entrepreneurial skills and commercial acumen and suggested to the HR team that I would be better off, and it would be more beneficial for the business, if I was placed in a position where I was building a new division. So they sent me to a state in India called Orissa which was plagued by unemployment, poor infrastructure and very minimal industrial development. My job was to build up the division of Coca-Cola there, with very little support, infrastructure or business processes.

And I loved it! I liked not having these support systems in place and at the age of 22 it is the closest I have come to setting up my own business. It really gave me a complete picture of business and how to operate in an environment externally where there are no established systems or ways of doing things. I realised I thrive under chaos; I love not having a rule book and creating some of the rules, building something new. I had lots of discretion and space to build networks, partnerships, go into society and see what they were doing and not doing . . . I had to engage with people, learn how to communicate in Oriya and see things from their point of view. It was critical to understand what type of relationship would work for both them and Coca-Cola.

I had no office and spent the first two years working out of a hot cramped local telephone booth. The owner was eventually kind enough to give me a chair and a part of his table. I convinced the booth operator to become a Coca-Cola distribution agent and today he is a dear friend and owns one of the largest and best distribution systems for Coca-Cola in Eastern India. I was able to make that decision based on instinctive judgement and hence I owe my first lessons on entrepreneurship and win–win business deals to a very ordinary telephone booth operator. This stint in my career really made me realise that I thrive on the sheer enormity of a challenge, with no direction, and like making my own way.

After a couple of years, when things were becoming more established, I started to get impatient. So I moved on to Unilever (then called Hindustan Lever Limited), another blue-chip company but very different – very organised and with strong support systems. I found the processes there constraining and only stayed two years. Unilever is a good employer, very professional and with robust systems, but it was a mismatch for how I operate; for me the processes took away individual contribution, uniqueness that individuals could bring. And so in early 2005 I moved on to work with Olam. I joined precisely because it sounded exciting and there was uncertainty about what needed to be done. In the interviews they said that I would be sent to Indonesia, to a region I had never heard of, and there would be challenging opportunities – my role would be to build the business and look for further business development opportunities. I would be in the cocoa business in Sulawesi, Indonesia and would need to be entrepreneurial, to say the least! My friends thought I had lost it – to leave a prized Mumbai posting to join some outfit and travel to some remote Indonesian island. But, relying on my instincts, I took the plunge. Now, years later, I can say that I had landed in the right place.

For four years I worked out of Olam's cocoa warehouse in Makassar, Indonesia as a business manager starting from the ground up. My main job was to increase purchase volumes of dry cocoa beans from Sulawesi (the third largest cocoa-growing location in the world). Very soon it became clear that generating this volume growth is easier said than done. Cocoa production in Indonesia was in serious trouble at that time from pests and disease. In my zeal to buy more cocoa I was spending at least 60% of my time on the ground, travelling in deep interiors for weeks at a time and this is when I got close to the farmers, the villagers. I would have dinner in the evening with the farmers' families or the village elders and got to see what the real issues were. I needed that closeness and in-depth understanding to be good at my job. Olam encouraged me to choose my own path for business development, to be entrepreneurial. At this time I started to realise that to make any progress we need to be credible with the farmers; one could not just come with ideas for the business development, but rather ideas of how the farmer would benefit in the longer term as well. We had to design a way to be close to the farm-gate and building value for them as well as us.

This experience really started to cement my ideas of what a good business model is, of creating win–win situations. Previous programmes by other companies had not worked because it was about building profit for the company alone and so when they stopped supporting the farmers . . . well, they were in trouble again. Other programmes were purely technical and run by NGOs [non-governmental organisation]/aid agencies but had no real market linkages; the farmer could not make a direct linkage between adopting good agricultural practices and improved income. So I had to re-engineer processes so that the programmes were beneficial to the farmer as well as us. We had to find a way where the farmer is successful, in the longer term, which helped our success. It is difficult to do this when there are no support systems, processes or manpower to do this sort of activity. Although I am entrepreneurial, I did learn from Unilever that proper support systems can really help to scale up projects.

An idea began to emerge of a programme to train farmers, but it had to be in a win–win way. I researched the idea in 2005, spoke with colleagues about it and got support and some resource commitment. A senior colleague from London was travelling in Indonesia at this time with an important customer and over an informal chat one evening the ideas of developing sustainable, traceable supply chain for cocoa really started to take shape. We got customer commitment and we started the programme with 120 farmer families, to train them on good agricultural practices focusing upon their needs. We started small, testing it out for six months. And it became really popular, with neighbouring farmers wanting to join. But we did not have the manpower, technical material and funding to scale it up and I realised that overcoming this bottleneck is where the real success of the programme lies – to scale it up.

In 2007 we approached USAID[2] [United States Agency for International Development] who were interested in an Indonesian programme targeting the agricultural sector with long-term impact after the funding period was over. To our good fortune, they contributed over US $1.8 million to beef up the programme and we extended it. Olam focused on developing the relationships – creating farmer groups and providing critical market linkage so the farmer got training and could sell his cocoa beans at a transparent and fair price. It was called the Amarta Programme and by 2010 it grew to include 22,000 farmer families. Now in 2012 it helps over 30,000 farmer families that we directly purchase cocoa beans from. It has been really successful and helped me achieve professional goals of sustainable business volumes while making a difference to the community around us. Olam now gets the best-quality cocoa, we give the fairest prices and get a stable and strong supply. The farmers are involved in sustainable farming practices and are likely to stay invested in their future as cocoa farmers.

I have to say I'm not a farmer and I don't have the technical skills of a farmer. But I understood the farmer, had a good working relationship and understood the context. I had an idea and saw the need and opportunity for that idea. To me this was not a charity thing; it is a business model, a business opportunity. It made sense to me and was a way to do my job successfully. That is what I am interested in: sustainable business models that create win–win opportunities for all. It's about recognising the need and creating an opportunity. While overall good for all participants in the chain has to be at the heart of the intention, I guess it was also critical to understand the bigger picture, the interlinkages between partners. But it would not have succeeded without business acumen, execution skills and some hard-headed determination at times – and most importantly, the support from Olam and USAID.

Being able to execute something like this is possible because I'm working in Olam. It is a company that is very much about 'Get on with it', with lots of trust and confidence in its people. Olam has an appetite for experimentation and even for failure. If we have about 20 of these programmes going on around the world, maybe only five will be successful – but these five grow exponentially and really help Olam to grow the rate it has grown and be the success it is. This entrepreneurial encouragement really benefits Olam and the spirit of experimentation gives this groundbreaking growth. This really excites and attracts the talent. It's about selecting the right people, putting them in the right place, letting them get on with it, empowering and trusting them, and directing them in what is right and wrong. The employees will then do what is right. I now have a team of over 300 people working out of various locations and believe that this entrepreneurial spirit attracts them to Olam. It's the ability to make a difference as an individual that is so important to me and that has made Olam successful.

My advice? Well, my entrepreneurial streak has been very important, and the freedom to do my work. The context at Olam to encourage, empower – this is so important. But it is critical to impact business and people at the same time, to understand this business model. Just doing business alone at the expense of people will not produce a sustainable or successful business. And execution of an idea is always more important than just the idea alone – good execution comes from understanding the context, putting in place the systems and processes that are needed and building good teams who are aligned.

Jo da Silva, Director, Arup (UK)

I went to work in Africa after the Rwanda genocide . . . in a situation like that you can make a difference. You see what human needs really are, and witness the stark reality that we have one planet which we've been using up rapidly . . . What I wanted to do is create something that can reach the people who need it most. People presumed this was philanthropy – I said no, this is about doing good business.

My father was in the British Foreign Office and I was born in Washington, DC (USA). My parents had pre-war and wartime values from a time when society was more community-focused and resource-aware. Certainly all my concerns about the environment are innate things from my childhood. We all had jobs from a young age, so quite young we learned you could earn money and use it to do what you wanted to do. I did not recognise it at the time, but putting back into society instead of taking was very ingrained in my values – we valued earning a living as opposed to making money.

At age 11 I went to boarding school in the UK. I wanted to study engineering at university because I loved making things. I studied at Cambridge University, helped by a bursary from the Institution of Civil Engineers as a result of an essay on the role of engineering in society. I thought that being an engineer was useful; engineers make a difference and benefit society. Throughout university I did various jobs so as to save money to travel in the summer vacations. I went to Israel, Jordan, Turkey, Egypt and India; I was fascinated by the different ways people lived.

After graduation I decided to go and live in India for a bit, simply because India was the most interesting place I'd come across. I got a job running a jungle camp which involved getting up at dawn every day and seeing tigers. I built a small clinic, a solar shower, a short stretch of road, an office and guest-house. That year after university was pivotal: catapulted from the UK to living in the jungle in India immersed in nature – raw and beautiful. In India you also see humanity every day; floodlit in three dimensions; dependent on a delicate balance with the environment. My thinking about society and the environment goes back to that year.

Back in the UK I started working for Arup as a graduate engineer. That was great because I enjoyed designing buildings, working with some of the top architects in the world and earning money. After two or three years, I moved to Hong Kong and worked on the design of the new Hong

Kong Airport, then briefly transferred to the Berlin office. Some time around then I came across RedR (www.redr.org). They're a charity that places engineers offering their professional skills in post-disaster situations. After the Iraq war in 1991, there was a call for engineer volunteers, I applied, was interviewed and accepted as a RedR member.

In 1994 I went to Tanzania on a RedR assignment after the Rwanda genocide with Concern, helping to construct refugee camps and improve roads to get food, medical supplies and stuff there. I wasn't fazed by Africa; it was not so different from India, although the genocide was a huge issue to deal with – I think I have seen more dead bodies than many professional soldiers. But in a situation like that you can make a difference, you see what human needs really are. You see the fragility of society; not just the genocide but also the fragility of human life afterwards; what it's like to be a human without access to water, and nowhere to shit with any privacy. It was an extraordinary few months. I lost my childhood innocence . . . saw poverty in the face, conflict, distrust but also immense amounts of hope and generosity.

After Rwanda I came back to Arup, once again working as a structural engineer. I was designing a building in Japan – a museum, a glass hemisphere just offshore in Osaka Bay, very high-tech, an amazing building. But I began to question things because Osaka is hot – we'd designed a greenhouse that needed loads of air conditioning yet I was concerned about the environment. At about that time I came across the Brundtland definition of sustainability (United Nations, 1987). The sustainability agenda made sense; the stark reality that we have one planet which we've been using up rapidly; and the equity side of it, billions of people in poverty but many others in obscene luxury; and dating back to the 1972 Club of Rome report (*The Limits to Growth*:[3] Meadows *et al.*, 1972) – people pointing out that economic growth is not a long-term strategy that's got a destination, rather it's a cul de sac. It brought everything together – my experiences in Rwanda, my job as an engineer building infrastructure to support human life. It mattered to be energy-efficient.

That was the beginning of the end of mainstream engineering for me, in order to focus on sustainable development. Happily I got a part-time fellowship at Sydney Sussex College, Cambridge University, one day a week so had some time to read, think, learn.

I was one of eight people who formed a task force in Arup to get sustainability on to Arup's agenda – the Sustainability Task Force. It was seeded by one board director who wanted to catalyse some activity. He invited 30 people globally to a workshop at Massachusetts Institute of Technology in Boston. Following that workshop, he approached the eight of us and asked if we would work together. We were junior management but this was the next generation's big agenda. He was looking for people to be activists.

I should explain . . . Arup was founded by a philosopher who was also an engineer [Sir Ove Nyquist Arup]. Social purpose, humanitarian attitude are core values – read his key speech.[4] He was 30–40 years ahead of his time, a real social entrepreneur. That's why I chose to work for them. They have a social conscience – you've got to make money but making money is not the raison d'être.

In the late '90s, beginning of 2000s, I was invited to set up a building engineering group and for several years I focused on social infrastructure for schools, libraries, museums – Sure Start, and the Academies programme.[5] Many of our clients were local authorities in deprived areas of town, and the sustainability of buildings was critical in terms of their social impact and operational costs, rather than their 'green' credentials.

The group was a success, and grew from six to about 30 people in three years but then the 2004 tsunami happened.[6] All this time I had continued with RedR after Rwanda, providing advice after disasters like Hurricane Mitch, but it was separate from my work life. When the tsunami happened, I was invited to work for UNHCR [United Nations High Commissioner for Refugees] to coordinate post-disaster shelter in Sri Lanka. The job description was very demanding – effectively coordinating shelter in-country with 100 NGOs. It brought together multiple threads of my career – my experiences as an engineer, understanding design and procurement, project management, experience of other post-disaster situations. I went for three months, but stayed for nine as there was a real job to do – we built 60,000 transitional shelters in six months.

After the tsunami I was at a crossroads – I'd had time to think. Who am I? What do I want to do? What mattered to me was that I have a skill set and perspective as an engineer, also some understanding, knowledge and experience of developing country contexts. What I wanted to do is create something that is a mechanism where the skills that exist with people like me, and the practices in Arup, can reach the people who need it most.

Arup is a company that's 10,000 people globally. We are the leading company in infrastructure in the built environment. But 80% of our work at that time was in developed-world countries. Sub-Saharan Africa and Asia is where there's scope to make much more impact. Rather than just designing buildings and bridges, we can create direct social impact by building sustainable communities.

I started with a feeling that this was the right thing to do, then researched how to substantiate that with an evidence base – how to create a viable business out of it? I wrote a paper to the chairman that was the beginning of an unsolicited conversation. I said the challenge for a firm like us is to think about how we can take our services to geographies where the issues we talk a lot about – climate change, energy, urbanisation – are prevalent. I said that a step to a solution is to have a small bit of the firm focused exclusively on working in developing countries on projects that contribute to social wellbeing and are sustainable in the environmental sense. This is about new approaches, new relationships – building a business within Arup from scratch.

I had supporters and non-supporters. There was lots of talking – some people didn't think it was relevant to the firm, others thought it was. It was about persuading key directors – I was lucky, I had two to three senior directors who believed in me. I thought about doing this on my own or with another organisation but there's a relationship between me and Arup – internal networks are as important as external networks.

You have to have clarity of purpose. For me, that clarity was building on trust in a long-term relationship. I was an insider coming in with a big idea that I could present in a business framework. The debate went on for months. People presumed this was philanthropy – I said, no, this is about doing good business. I drew a diagram that explained the spectrum running from philanthropy to major business opportunity. I was asked to present this at the Annual Group Meeting to the directors and that's where I got the endorsement. People could see this was not just about spending the firm's money but about investing in a new business area that would have long-term business benefits.

I was pushed to present a clear business plan from the outset. I said: 'I can't because I'm asking for investment to be able to write a meaningful business plan'. My business case was back-analysis of attempts to win work in this sector – over the last 12 months the firm had wasted thousand pounds on pursuing work that had come to nothing. I said, instead of wasting that money, let's think harder. I did do a lot of looking at other companies and talking – for example, to Gib Bulloch at ADP [Accenture Development Partnerships],[7] who was really helpful.

The first year or so was difficult. I was operating within another business, on their business model. As of 1 April [2010] Arup International

Development (ArupID) became its own profit-and-loss centre reporting directly to the board. I got made a director as well – which was important for credibility. Year by year you have to climb through the system – ArupID is a declared not-for-profit (NFP) entity in the firm. Perhaps next year I'll be a distinct trading entity – a NFP – owned by the Arup Group but distinct.

Managing expectations is important – just understanding the deal between my bit of the business and the business overall. And expectations aren't easily measurable. Getting clarity on expectation is important, so nine months into a financial year I can say: 'This is what I've been doing and I've exceeded expectations'. Part of that is finance but we have also built key strategic relationships that provide opportunities – the intangibles and the tangibles.

There are many days I think, why did I do this? But it's in my character. It's my contribution.

3.2 The Social Intrapreneur

Very little is written on Social Intrapreneurs, the starting point being work by academics Meyerson (2001), who identified a type of employee called 'Tempered Radicals': employees who identify with their organisations but are also committed to a cause or ideology that is fundamentally different to the dominant culture of their organisation. They successfully 'walk the tightrope' between conformity and rebellion by sticking to their values, assert their agendas and create change without jeopardising their careers (Meyerson, 2001). John Elkington, thought leader in sustainability and expert on social entrepreneurs, followed up this work in 2008 with a field guide called *The Social Intrapreneur: A Field Guide for Change-Makers*.

These initial works highlighted some unique characteristics that this new type of employee has: change-makers thinking outside the standard norms with strong social values that they refuse to compromise on at work and (as John Elkington especially highlights) with a determination to create both social and financial good. Social Intrapreneurs prefer to do this with their employers because they believe business should be a force for good. These employees respect and enjoy the business world and the challenges and complexities of for-profit organisations, but believe that the fundamental business model needs to be one that creates win–win situations for all.

my ideas of what a good business model is, of creating win–win situations. Just doing business at the expense of business is not doing business right, not doing it sustainably. We need to impact business and society at the same time.

(Sumanta, Olam)

Social Intrapreneurs are unique in that they view business as inclusive[8] within society and the environment, not separate from them. Both Sumanta (Olam) and Jo (Arup) talk honestly about how logical it is to them that business must be inclusive within society and environmental boundaries, but Jo especially talks of the difficulty in getting others to understand this mindset – of having to explain why this is good business sense and not philanthropy. It is a brave position to take as it is usually pushing against the status quo, can be disruptive and, in the wrong organisation, it can jeopardise careers.

However, Social Intrapreneurs can also create a significant and wide-scale positive impact on society and business.

The Doughty Centre team identified six types of Social Intrapreneurs (Grayson *et al.*, 2011):

1. Resigned: left their company because of a lack of support for their ideas
2. Frustrated: remain within the company but have given up pushing for social innovation
3. Emergent: starting out with their ideas and still unclear how the corporate environment will respond
4. Quiet: operating below the corporate radar in order not to attract criticism or objections
5. Tolerated: experimenting with ideas while the company is indifferent or neutral towards their activities
6. Embraced: the company is actively encouraging their ideas, empowering them.

Social Intrapreneurs may experience several of these stages, in a non-linear route, often because of the stage of life and career they are in, the organisation they are working for, and because of the wider socioeconomic and political environment. For example, Sumanta – while working for Olam – could be 'Embraced' by Olam, who prize entrepreneurship from their employees and support experimentation. Jo (Arup) could initially be described as having gone from Emergent (her initial idea for ArupID) to Tolerated (given three months to develop a business plan) to Embraced (made Director and now a declared not-for-profit within Arup).

I started with a feeling that this was the right thing to do, then researched how to substantiate that with an evidence base, how to create a viable business out of it.

('Emergent' Jo, Arup)

Table 3.1 Example activities of Social Intrapreneurs

New product or service	Creation of micro-insurance products for low-income people and businesses unable to afford conventional insurance schemes Development of a micro-energy project within a major energy generation corporation to boost productivity and address poverty in developing countries Development of 'sustainable information technology' service streams at a major engineering company
New business unit	Start-up of a business unit within a large parcel delivery corporation to improve operational efficiency whilst ameliorating climate change impacts Launch of an alternative energy business within a major oil company to service customers in emerging markets
Innovative technology scale-up	Development of commercially viable irrigation technology to address water shortages in desert environments, which could be exported to other countries
Process change	Reduction of a large brewing company's production costs to improve competitiveness in developing countries through partnerships with local growers Engineering of environmentally sustainable production processes at a global chemicals company
Introduce new business models, including collaborative working	Creation of a coalition within a major energy provider to address problems of fuel poverty Establishment of environmental sustainability coalitions and projects in a global management consultancy Creation of partnerships to leverage and develop management expertise in developing countries

Social Intrapreneurs create innovations, whether new business divisions, projects, products, changing sourcing or operations, redesigning engineering processes, influencing strategy or changing business processes to overcome an issue affecting multiple stakeholders. Some do this within their existing role; others expand their role or create a new role with their company in order to run a project. Critically, they may:

1. Rectify social inequalities through inclusive business solutions and/or
2. Re-engineer business processes to improve resource management and mitigate environmental impacts (Table 3.1).

Thus, as well as creators of innovation, Social Intrapreneurs as an employee type can be seen as a form of innovation, where employees are proactively creating new ways of doing business with unique mindsets of the role business has in society. Innovation is commonly defined as improved or new technology, products, services and ways of doing things:

improvements in technology and better methods or ways of doing things.

(Professor M Porter, 1990)

Professors Porter and Kramer talk further about social innovation – new strategies, concepts and ideas that meet social needs, whether health, community development or workers' rights – in relation to how they view the role of business in society: as creating 'shared value'.[9] This is similar to how many Social Intrapreneurs describe what they see as the right business model:

> Policies and operating practices that enhance the competitiveness of a company while simultaneously advancing the economic and social conditions in the communities in which it operates. Shared value creation focuses on identifying and expanding the connections between societal and economic progress.
>
> (Porter and Kramer, 2011)

Social movement theory emerged from the research as a key explanation for why new types of employees pushing for social change are emerging now (Fuchs, 2006). However, whereas this certainly may apply to Social Intrapreneurs, what employees such as Jo (Arup) and Sumanta (Olam) uniquely do is create entire new products, services, departments and ways of working that can be disruptive – disruptive social innovation.

Social innovation can be incremental (when a series of small improvements occur over time, the most common type of innovation) or radical (when something new is created that specifically can *disrupt* the way we do things or think of things). Disruptive innovation can have a positive or negative impact on the current status quo. Social Intrapreneurs themselves can be seen as a disruptive force – because of their new way of thinking and doing. Academic Mayer Zald called those who move against the social norms to create new policies and practices 'bureaucratic insurgents': a relatively small group of middle managers and professionals working to change products, processes or policies partially from within. He argues these professionals have a different perspective on the possibilities that exist than the higher authorities in the organisation (Zald, 2005). The change the insurgents create can have a positive or negative impact, but critically insurgency can be prosocial (prosocial bureaucratic insurgency: when the efforts serve societal and organisational interests) – as seen with Social Intrapreneurs.

However, despite Social Intrapreneurs themselves being an innovation, it is worth noting that they often find success because they actually adopt an incremental approach to creating social innovation – although they create new processes, products or services, they utilise existing business resources and projects and ground their efforts in proven business acumen. Jo (Arup), for example, successfully set up an operational division after first defining the resource need, outcomes and benefits to the business and a business plan –

all typical ways of doing business when setting up a new service/division/product.

> This is about doing good business . . . about investing in a new business area that would have long-term business benefits . . . I could present that in a business framework.
>
> (Jo, Arup)

Thus, as a new employee type, Social Intrapreneurs can be prosocial bureaucratic insurgents (as a manifestation of disruptive social innovation) – but the methods they employ within business could be seen as incremental innovation. These methods are described later in this chapter.

3.3 Understanding the Social Intrapreneur

All the Social Intrapreneurs interviewed recounted memorable childhood experiences where they were exposed to and learned about community, social or environmental-based issues. These childhood experiences significantly contribute to the priorities they have in adulthood.[10]

> I was born in one of the poorest states in India. In my childhood I saw lots of people well below the poverty line, struggling. Farmers were moving into cities but still not earning enough.
>
> (Sumanta, Olam)

These experiences influenced their individual values and characteristics:

> I went to Jesuit schools, and now realise that unconsciously some of these principles of simplicity and hard work did influence my values.
>
> (Sumanta, Olam)

These early learned experiences and shaping of values can influence the prioritisation Social Intrapreneurs place on what they want to achieve through work, e.g. social and economic value creation over pure income generation and promotion. However, as with the other change-makers profiled in this book, Social Intrapreneurs also display a clear understanding of who they are – they have a clear self-identity. More specifically, they are clear on the contribution they uniquely want to make in the world (Visser, 2008).[11] This can be because they – as with most people – want to understand the meaning of their life (scientist Viktor Frankl's theory of meaning of life and how work can be a source because it helps us experience our values and enact deeds – Frankl, 1964) and because they want to understand their unique place and identity in the world (Freud's theory of ego and id); their 'meaning of life'. When that moment of clarity is experienced – of finding a source that contributes to that meaning or conversely realising what you are doing does not contribute to that meaning – it can be memorable:

> It brought everything together – my experiences in Rwanda, my job as an engineer building infrastructure to support human life. It mattered to be energy-efficient. That was the beginning of the end of mainstream engineering for me.
>
> (Jo, Arup)

This clarity of self can also reinforce one's self-belief and determination to succeed with related ventures (Bansal, 2003; Hemingway and Maclagan, 2004), provide a determination to develop the ideas, work hard to succeed and reinforce the self-belief that the related efforts are the correct course of action (Parker *et al.*, 2010). The ventures Social Intrapreneurs build are a representation of their personal mindset, values and behaviours.

> Where there's a will there's a way.
>
> (Jo, Arup)

3.3.1 A unique mindset

As previously discussed, Social Intrapreneurs have a unique mindset in how they view the role of business in society. They have overcome the traditional dichotomy of thinking in terms of 'either/or' for how business and society interact and see business as interconnected and dependent on the wellbeing of society and the environment, and vice versa. This way of thinking may not be always apparent to them and many initially struggle in a corporate environment where they may be pigeon-holed as advocating philanthropy; or struggle in a not-for-profit environment where for-profit business purpose is not a driver of operations. This could be why many of those who are not encouraged or enabled by their organisations tend to leave (the 'Frustrated' or 'Resigned') and many become social entrepreneurs, creating a business where they can pursue their view of the role of business in society.

Often, as with the case for Sumanta (Olam), Social Intrapreneurs do not see the way they view the role of business in society as unique; rather this mindset fits completely with their personal values and early learned experiences. Many state they simply see the correct route that business should take, the logical route given the sustainability problems faced by humankind. However, this is still a unique way of thinking – very much long-term, inclusive and sustainable – and Social Intrapreneurs work hard to maintain and practise that mindset, actively looking for where societal and business benefit intersect.

This experience really started to cement my ideas of what a good business model is, of creating win–win situations . . . To me this was not a charity thing, it is a business model, a business opportunity. That is what I am interested in; creating sustainable business models that create win–win opportunities for all.

(Sumanta, Olam)

3.3.2 An entrepreneurial spirit

It is no coincidence that the term 'Intrapreneur' derives from 'Entrepreneur'. The personal characteristics and skill set of a Social Intrapreneur are similar to those of a social entrepreneur. Social entrepreneurs:

are ambitious and persistent, taking major social issues and offering new ideas for wide-scale change . . . they find what is not working and solve the problem by changing the solution, and persuading entire societies to take new leaps.

(Ashoka, 2010)

Similar to Social Intrapreneurs, entrepreneurs see opportunities to provide new solutions; have moments of inspiration; will take direct action; and are creative, have courage and fortitude – characteristics fundamental to innovation (Martin and Osberg, 2007).

My entrepreneurial streak has been very important, and the freedom to do my work.

(Sumanta, Olam)

The research showed that Social Intrapreneurs also have:

- A strong learning orientation: whether intellectual curiosity for their subject area and/or wider macro-level issues, Social Intrapreneurs exhibit a strong learning orientation, mostly expressing an experiential experience that involved trial and error. The learning opportunities often emerged from their contact with the communities they want to help.
- The flexibility to create 'space' within their work, often in isolation, to think, reflect and learn – but then able to work closely within a team the next day:

Happily I got a part-time fellowship at Sydney Sussex College, Cambridge University, one day a week so had some time to read, think, learn.

(Jo, Arup)

- The skill set to engage with others to gather ideas, share insights and learn from their peers. Collaborative relationships are important for gathering ideas and learning, both with other parts of the business and also with external collaborators. This requires the skills of listening, communicating ideas well and engaging with many different types of people with different opinion, insights and perspectives.

It is important however to remember the key difference between social entrepreneurs and Social Intrapreneurs (Makhlouf, 2011): social entrepreneurs are pursuing a 'social mission' and take direct action by creating a social organisation that can pursue that social mission using business principles and disciplines. Social Intrapreneurs – especially those with a purpose specific to sustainability – are pursuing a mission that is both social and for profit, and work from within existing commercial organisations.

3.4 Advice for Social Intrapreneurs

The most notable enablers for Social Intrapreneurs are the business skills and acumen that help them to be successful. Whether this is specialist technical knowledge related to their cause (such as Jo at Arup and architectural sustainable development, or Sumanta with business scale-up skills gained working at Coca-Cola) or all-round business acumen, they rely on solid business skills gained from past work experiences.

> It is the closest I have come to setting up my own business. It really gave me a complete picture of business and how to operate in an environment externally where there are no systems or ways of doing things.
>
> (Sumanta, Olam)

This business acumen is essential, firstly to identify the opportunity for a business to create a new product/service with societal value; secondly because of the business skills they need to develop the idea and then take it to operational scale; and also because of the credibility and trust Social Intrapreneurs need to earn from their supporters to get their idea sanctioned. Being close to both the issues being addressed and to the business can also help identify opportunities – to see the real limitations and opportunities that will face the business.

> starting from the ground up . . . you really need to be credible and get on with the farmers; you could not just come with ideas for the business, but ideas of how the farmer would benefit in the longer term. How we could add value for them. And I could see how the poor could benefit.
>
> (Sumanta, Olam)

These entrepreneurial skills, combined with a deep knowledge of their business, helped the Social Intrapreneurs to gain the trust of their employer. This trust is essential for the necessary leeway to experiment with new ideas and to gain the support of key corporate decision-makers who determine strategy and have the power to invest resources in social innovation projects.

Thus, budding Social Intrapreneurs could:

1. Spend time developing deep business acumen, to understand the real-world limitations and opportunities, and the practicalities of scaling up an idea. Encourage the entrepreneurial impulses and get grounded experience in creating or building a new project, service or department.
2. Expose themselves to the issues, not from a desk in another country, but on the ground. This is when it becomes easier to make connections, understand the interactions and pressures and engage with the very stakeholders involved:

> to understand what is going on at ground level, the complexity of the context is so important.
>
> (Sumanta, Olam)

3. Build up credibility in the business and earn the trust of senior members of the organisation. This will be critical when pitching ideas and looking for support and allies.
4. Have an ability to find and inspire others in the organisation to champion them or at least to give them access and a platform to pitch their ideas. Networking and engaging with internal stakeholders can be very useful.
5. Seize an idea and persist with it: direct advice given by the Social Intrapreneurs was needing persistence to follow through ideas, often when co-workers in the organisation did not understand or support their mindset. As with Sustainability Specialists, there is a need to be resilient and have 'dogged determination'.

Other common skills among Social Intrapreneurs include communication with co-workers and stakeholders (aiding in building the trust that Social Intrapreneurs need to earn in order to pursue their ideas) and marketing skills (whether presentation, persuasion or story-telling, this appears to help build a business case for a project and engage the support of others).

> I wrote a paper to the chairman that was the beginning of an unsolicited conversation. I said the challenge for a firm like us is to think about how we can take our services to geographies where the issues we talk a lot about – climate change, energy, urbanization – are prevalent.
>
> (Jo, Arup)

Social Intrapreneurs also appear skilled at working in partnership with other organisations, whether exploring an idea or finding ways to scale up a project. Such partnerships can expose Social Intrapreneurs to alternative solutions and gain the expertise needed, or provide external validation for their programmes. There are numerous examples of collaborative relationships with other parts of the organisation as well as with NGOs, governing bodies, educational institutions and commercial organisations – all benefiting their projects in various ways. These external groups can be significant enablers for Social Intrapreneurs – whether business schools, NGOs, corporate responsibility coalitions or foundations and venture capitalists.

3.4.1 The development journey

The Social Intrapreneur's journey of developing an idea into a feasible and workable venture has been described by Maggie Brenneke[12] as passing through several stages to get ideas active:

1. Inspire: 'aha' moment – the idea emerges. This typically can occur during an on-site experience or after an issue has emerged and there is a need for a platform to address that whilst creating business success.
2. Design: research the idea. This is when strong business skills and a deep understanding of the issue, stakeholders, and limitations and opportunities become critical.
3. Lift: find finance, mentors, allies, momentum. Sumanta and Jo both engaged other members of their organisation to find advice on how to finance, and build internal support for the idea.
4. Launch: test and perhaps go to scale. Social Intrapreneurs encourage other employees and stakeholders on to the project, creating a team around them to take the idea to a workable scale that could have real impact.
5. Scale: take the intrapreneurial idea from test-market to broad scale. This is again where working in collaboration with others (for example, USAID for Sumanta) and applying sound business skills are real advantages.

We see this process work with both Jo (Arup) and Sumanta (Olam) and a useful framework to emulate. Sumanta, for example:

1. had an inspirational moment (i.e. the formation of the idea for Sumanta when visiting the cocoa farmers);
2. researched the idea for feasibility and if it fit as a win–win model;
3. found colleagues to help (lift) and USAID to support with resource;
4. launched the programme (initially to a small group of farmers);
5. and then took the programme to scale and now supports over 30,000 farmer families with the skills needed to sustain their farms and livelihoods.

3.4.2 Power

Power (the ability to wield authority and take action, such as making decisions, utilising resources, influencing people and initiating projects – often derived from rank or position) is a significant enabler for any change-maker in an organisation – more so for Social Intrapreneurs, because as change-makers they are introducing mindset and actions that could be contrary to the status quo and therefore not often welcomed or understood. Consider the process Jo at Arup underwent to show why her idea was relevant to the business – essential for her to do because she did not have the positional power simply to take action and set up a new division, and in this example Jo did have a Godparent helping (see Chapter 5). However, personal authority is essential for Social Intrapreneurs to develop. Authority is the right and authorisation to wield power, or to influence others who have power to take action. Social Intrapreneurs may often not have the power they need but can develop the authority they need to make decisions, utilise resources and take action. Power can then be earned, such as Jo earning the status of Director for ArupID, which gives her the power to make decisions.

There are four broad types of power available to Social Intrapreneurs to use:

1. *Borrowed*: power inherent in the organisation's system, such as rank, which can be lent to a Specialist for a period of time (Balogun *et al.*, 2005). Further, if the organisational leader sanctions the Social Intrapreneur to take action, then authority can be 'lent' to the change-maker to carry out that change (Zald, 2005). This is in part why it is so important to have active Chief Executive Officer support. Godparents can also often 'lend' power (explored in Chapter 5).

2. *Earned authority*: Social Intrapreneurs may not yet have enough positional power or authority but, because of good past performance and relationships, they have earned credibility and therefore the moral authority (Lawrence *et al.*, 2006) to take action and be supported by those with the authority.

3. *Positional power*: this is when the Social Intrapreneur already has a senior position embedded within the system of the organisation, with resources such as budget and an authentic and powerful reporting line, such as a Director or C-suite role (Balogun *et al.*, 2005). Alternatively, it can be when the Social Intrapreneur has been given a position with power (earned power) specific to that individual's work as a Social Intrapreneur – such as Jo being given the status of Director for ArupID, which gives her the power to make decisions and manage resources.

4. The fourth type of power – *entrepreneurial* power – is when managers take power without permission in order to carry out their job.[13] This can be by enlisting a powerful stakeholder and promising action that then needs to be fulfilled by the organisation, or arguing the case for their idea so effectively that they are given discretion to scope out the idea as a new enterprise. This is a common tactic for Social Intrapreneurs that works well. However, this can be disruptive (in a negative or positive way) and resonates with the idea that Social Intrapreneurs are in themselves a form of innovation (discussed earlier). Borrowing or giving change-makers some power to do things can be more constructive and

preferable, especially when the power is clearly directed to the corporate agenda (Zald, 2005).

> It was about persuading key directors – I was lucky, I had two to three senior directors who believed in me. I thought about doing this on my own or with another organisation but there's a relationship between me and Arup – internal networks are as important as external networks.
>
> (Jo, Arup)

3.5 Advice for organisations

Empowered Social Intrapreneurs can be very beneficial for organisations as loyal employees and also in introducing innovation into the organisation's mindset and products/services. They can help the organisation achieve sustainability goals, enhance colleague motivation and talent, help engage other employees in sustainability, introduce innovation into the organisation and improve the reputation of the organisation through successful ventures. However, because they are a relatively new type of employee, sometimes managers or the organisation as a whole may not recognise them, understand their potential or nurture them. There is no formal job description for a Social Intrapreneur; this can be a positive thing in that there are no preconceived restrictions to stifle experimentation, but this lack of recognition can also hinder progress as the role can be unrecognised and unpredictable and require new skill sets not present in the organisation, such as stakeholder management, entrepreneurial skills and transparency management (BITC, 2012).

3.5.1 Typical obstacles

Responses to Social Intrapreneurs, specifically from co-workers, line managers, organisational leaders or HR systems, can span from active rejection, ignorance, indifference, accidentally smothering to mature empowerment. Typical obstacles include:

- Direct line managers or middle and senior managers not understanding what, why and how Social Intrapreneurs work. This could be grounded in misunderstanding what sustainability means, short-term thinking, lack of exposure to sustainability thinking or limited understanding of the role of business in society as either/or.
- Obstructive politics within the organisation and limited sharing of power, authority and responsibility. For example, with difficulty releasing corporate assets, other business priorities seen as more important, no senior sponsor from someone who has power or inappropriate scale of how the organisation measures returns and key performance indicators of what success is.

- Leaders of the organisation don't clearly communicate what is 'on' or 'off' the corporate agenda (what is considered to be relevant to the business) or communicate a restricted agenda that is not open to discussion. This can discourage 'managerial discretion'[14] to identify new opportunities or risks. A clearly communicated organisational agenda (Bansal, 2003) is critical, but mechanisms that allow the agenda to be discussed will give permission for employees such as Social Intrapreneurs to identify and seek permission to raise opportunities or risks they spot. In a few circumstances, if the corporate agenda is too restricted then negative bureaucratic insurgency can arise.
- Policies and procedures within the organisation that may stifle or restrict Social Intrapreneurs. These systems may have been put in place to support employee types who prefer a structured regimen, but this can be very counterproductive for Social Intrapreneurs, who tend to need 'space' to think, reflect, consult and design. Line managers can be significantly helpful by allowing Social Intrapreneurs the 'space' to reflect and experiment. See Chapter 5 (Godparents) for examples of this.

> another blue-chip company but very different. Very organised with strong support systems. I found the processes there too constraining . . . it was a mismatch for how I operate; for me the processes took away individual contribution . . . I could not be entrepreneurial.
>
> (Sumanta, Olam)

3.5.2 Organisational culture

The culture of an organisation (why and how the company does business: 'The way things get done around here' – Deal and Kennedy, 1982) can be a powerful enabler or blocker if, for example, it discourages entrepreneurial thinking, if there are embedded barriers to cross-department working such as silo thinking or if the organisation is very risk- and experimentation-adverse. Sumanta stresses the importance of the organisational culture as enabling or blocking Social Intrapreneurs:

> Being able to execute something like this is possible because I'm working in Olam . . . It is a company that is very much about 'Get on with it', with lots of discretion, trust and confidence in its people. Olam has an appetite for experimentation, and even for failure . . . the entrepreneurial and experimentation gives the groundbreaking growth . . . The context at Olam to encourage, empower is so important.
>
> (Sumanta, Olam)

However, 'culture' is often not the responsibility of one person or team, nor seen as a specific asset to be developed so that it enables employees and business success. Individual elements that make up the culture could include 'tone from the top', which is the tone leaders of the organisation set through their words, stories they tell and priorities they emphasise which can directly motivate employees and answer what its place in the world is. For an example of an organisation that strategically develops its culture, see Chapter 1 (Unsung Heroes).

3.5.3 Support for the Social Intrapreneur

Any single organisation will have a few different 'types' of employees working within its ranks, motivated and taking action for very different reasons. Good HR specialists recognise this and structure 'reward packages' with a standard offering of salary in exchange for an employee's contribution, with additional rewards that can be adapted to what motivates a particular employee – because different employees seek different types of rewards from their workplace (Net Impact, 2012). For example, pay brackets may be graded and standardised but discretion given to managers for where within the grade an employee sits depending on how well he or she does in 360-degree feedback.[15]

In a *total* reward package, however, pay is only one element. Training and development, recognition, networking opportunities, flexible working conditions, time built into their job to experiment, collaboration opportunities and project-based opportunities all contribute to a total reward package which can be adapted to the context of an employee's working situation, motivation and relationship with the organisation (Williamson *et al.*, 2009). Interpersonal trust and a supportive learning culture specifically can motivate employees and enhance their commitment to the organisation (Song and Kim, 2008). This sort of approach is especially relevant for how organisations can reward and motivate Social Intrapreneurs.

Social Intrapreneurs do not operate in a vacuum, rather within a collective – or an eco-system – with other members of that collective. As much as organisational leaders need to do, HR professionals and direct managers can understand and encourage Social Intrapreneurs. So too can Sustainability Specialists. Specialists can act as catalysts (a source for igniting their potential), mentors, champions or technical experts. They can proactively encourage Social Intrapreneurs to join external networks and online mutual support groups, and develop programmes with the Learning and Development teams such as learning to network, communicating and presenting, and building allies. Specialists can initiate partnering programmes, where a senior member of the organisation partners a Social Intrapreneur so that both can learn from the other (see Dynamic Duos in Chapter 5, Godparents). Volunteer schemes, run by either the HR or Sustainability Specialists, can also help by giving opportunities for Social Intrapreneurs to utilise their professional expertise in a social capacity and also gain firsthand experiences of how business can contribute to social need.

3.6 Concluding thoughts

The context of an organisation is critical for enabling Social Intrapreneurs, such as the messages sent and tone set by leaders; the culture of the organisation; and the actions of HR, Specialists and direct line managers in enabling Social Intrapreneurs. However, key is to remember the individual – the person behind the label. Jo – who says she has probably seen more dead bodies than most serving soldiers and is determined to bring engineering into the social value creation space – and Sumanta – who moved to a place he had never heard of and ended up helping over 30,000 farmer families gain the skills needed to keep their businesses alive – are real people striving to create a better society. Their passion and motivation are clear. There are clear common characteristics, experiences, values and outlooks among all the Social Intrapreneurs studied. However, further research could highlight the breadth of these employees across the globe, and understand if they are part of the sustainability social movement, or new manifestations of social innovation – or both.

3.6.1 Summary advice

Be self-aware: don't start unless you are prepared to see it through, but don't think you need all the answers before you start:

- How important is the idea to me?
- How much personal time and energy am I prepared to invest?
- In terms of my discretionary time to push things that matter to me, where am I likely to have most effect?

Marshall your case:

- Can I make a compelling business case for action relevant to the stage of corporate responsibility maturity of the company?
- How would my project save money/make money, build reputation or otherwise be beneficial for the business? How will it have a positive impact on the environment/society?
- Can it help to advance any existing corporate programmes and, therefore, could the idea be linked to these to make adoption easier?

Recruit supporters and neutralise opponents:

- Where can I find champions and 'sponsors' who can provide 'air cover', release resources and promote my ideas up the organisation?
- Have I anticipated and understood any opposition and can I either address or counter their arguments?

Be persistent:

- Am I prepared for reverses and rejections?
- Am I prepared to carry on when others say 'no'? Could I modify my proposal so as to neutralise objections when I meet them?

Keep up momentum:

- Once the project is developed, am I prepared to hand it over to others to keep it running?
- How will I ensure that my project will survive and prosper after I've moved on to another project or company?

3.7 Further reading

Grayson D, Spitzeck H, Alt E, McLaren M (2011). *Social Intrapreneurs – An Extra Force for Sustainability.* Cranfield: Cranfield University.

Marshall J, Coleman G, Reason P (2011). *Leadership for Sustainability.* Sheffield: Greenleaf.

Meyerson D (2001). *Tempered Radicals. How People Use Difference to Inspire Change at Work.* Boston: Harvard Business Press, USA.

Visser W (2008). *Making A Difference: Purpose-Inspired Leadership for Corporate Sustainability and Responsibility (CSR).* Saarbrücken: VDM.

4   The Sustainability Champion

Champion: (noun) a person who vigorously supports or defends a person or cause; (verb) supporting, defending or fighting for a person, belief, right or principle enthusiastically.

There have always been champions of one sort or another in organisations, supporting a cause that could be personal to them, or formally nominated to be a champion for a change programme. The specific development of Sustainability Champions has grown rapidly over the last decade from an ad hoc group of individual employees to what may be a professional internal network of champions across the business with objectives, a support structure, resources and specific responsibilities.

Sustainability Champions are employees who support the efforts being made to create a sustainable organisation, often helping to implement change within their own sphere of influence, and in some instances initiating change across the organisation. They do this mainly as an addition to their day job, sometimes working overtime or unofficially. Without these champions the Specialists would not be as effective, and in fact possibly fail in their task. Champions tend to be effective in what they do because they are embedded across the business, with access, trust, moral authority and business know-how.

The first part of this chapter shares some best-practice examples of Sustainability Champions, giving an insight into what they do, how, and, importantly, why. They share their personal stories of why being a Sustainability Champion represents the type of person they are. The second part of the chapter explores their skills, competencies and motivations and then gives advice on how Champions can be encouraged and enabled, especially through a support structure such as a network. The stories of the Champions reveal passionate, loyal and caring employees who have found a way to express their values and be part of creating a more responsible organisation. Hopefully many of you will recognise yourselves in these stories, or are inspired to combine the job you love doing with your personal values and desires. Sustainability Champions around the globe truly are changing the world without losing their day job – by taking action from *inside* their organisations.

4.1 Case studies

Wouter van der Bank, Logistics Manager, Reed Elsevier (Netherlands)

I have been at Reed Elsevier since 1979 . . . I am loyal to them and they are loyal to me. I like helping others, I like sharing best practice. I know I have credibility and know the business really well . . . I do enjoy what we do!

I think I came to sustainability later in life, because in truth it was not something that drove me in my childhood or early career. I was always interested in politics, as a left-wing Socialist in Amsterdam in the 1970s, and I've done demonstrations against nuclear and chemical waste – but sports is what interested me at school. I am more aware now, both at work where it interests me and at home where I encourage my youngest daughter to grow her own vegetables.

I joined Reed Elsevier straight from school, in 1979, and have worked with them ever since. So yes, you could say I am a loyal person! I have worked my way up at Reed Elsevier, from working in the warehouse, Mailing, Printing, Marketing, to Facilities. I feel at home here, it is a big company with lots of opportunities and they really invest in me. I'm loyal to them and they are loyal to me. I push myself to advance and they push me to advance.

I first joined the Green Team because my manager asked me and it is difficult for me to say no. I am also on the Incident Management and the Business Continuity teams and a first aider! But I did recognise that someone on Facilities needed to be on the Green Team because we can facilitate actions, get things done. I like being able to get things done and I think I am trusted to be the person who can get things done. I'm the type of person that, if I take something on, I will do it to my best ability. I'm not afraid to talk and organise – no matter what my rank is. I have pride in what I do. This is true with the Green Team.

We have issues, for example the Green Team I am a member of in Amsterdam is special but it is not representative of some other teams across the business because the cultures of divisions are different. But everywhere some employees care, others don't and this can be negative. But I don't let that stop me doing things. One day, with support from Head of Facilities and the board, we turned the heat down one degree. There were positive and negative reactions and you deal with that. What it does do is get people talking, thinking. I organised a 'Walk the Stairs' week where we said don't use the elevator, and designed the stairs as keys on a piano – that helped change behaviour and being able to do that is good.[1] The Sustainability team in Head Office in the UK send us ideas, and we have our own ideas that we come up with and run many activities to get employees thinking, talking and hopefully change their behaviour. Many of the activities I can do because of where I work, because I have access to budget, and because people at Reed Elsevier know me and I have credibility from my experience here.

Some activities have failed because a past manager was a bit too cautious. This was sometimes frustrating but I understood it was because he did not yet have the right authority. I did not change how I did things – I have always felt comfortable with what we do. That manager left and I got a manager who is supportive. My department is aware of what I do and some are interested and some are not. But by them knowing – they are unconsciously involved!

The people in the Green Team make it a success, with support from Head Office and from my direct manager. Personally, I take pride in what I do. And it's nice to know, motivating to know that people take seriously what I do. It is nice that people notice. I like sharing what we do with other divisions at Reed Elsevier and I like helping others.

Priya Dandawate, Program Manager, Microsoft (USA)

You can bulldoze over the environment, or you can interact with it; I know which I prefer. I'm an engineer, I love building and creating. I am part of a bigger global grassroots movement that is very important – if we don't take care of this planet we will die.

I was born in Detroit, USA, which is a blue-collar city in the mid-west with lots of immigrants and plenty of open spaces and corn fields. My parents are first-generation Indians so we travelled a lot to India when I was a child. I had a foot in two very different worlds and the contrast between the first and third world was significant – I could see how fortunate we were in the US but I could also see how important religion, impact and resource use was in India. In India, careful use of resource is part of living, whereas in the US we are a very wasteful society. At the time I did not know what to do with the feelings this evoked but now I see this is where my interest in conserving resources, and the impact of resources on economic development, stems from.

I vividly remember a programme on US television that I used to watch as a child with all my friends – *Captain Planet*. Each week *Captain Planet and the Planeteers*[2] had an environmental challenge to overcome to save the environment. I loved that show! I was probably an unusual child, I loved being outside collecting bugs but I also loved being on the computer. When we moved to Washington DC though it was harder to play outside, and was a huge shock culturally – it's a very rich county and people cared about different things, wealth was seen differently.

At 18 I took a year off and went to study in Germany. Germany is so different. Recycling and environmental action is ingrained in the home, in everyday actions. It's not seen as a burden, but something as normal as cleaning your teeth. I think this is where I realised that to help people to change you have to make it easy, a normal part of their behaviour. I got the bug for travelling though and have since travelled around the world a few times. Nepal and Bangkok was amazing for showing me how important basic resources are, such as water. Being able to see how different cultures interact with the environment was a key lesson for me – you can bulldoze over the environment or you can interact with it, which is the more innovative approach.

I always loved building things, creating things and always knew I wanted to be an engineer. I took Engineering at university and loved the sciences and physics, although it was not till later that I saw how that can be applied to the environment. I became a vegetarian, strongly influenced by my Indian background and Hindu belief that taking a life is an important thing and to only be done with great consideration.

I knew I wanted to work for Microsoft in year 2 of my degree – I had used their products all my life! Bill Gates is an inspiration, so innovative, and now he is successful giving back so much. I eventually got a job there and have stayed. I am privileged to work for Microsoft, it's a unique culture. We make the connection between engineering and the environment – in a different culture that does not make this connection it could get demoralising. Being based in Seattle helps as well, as Seattle is very environmentally aware for a US city. But Microsoft encourages entrepreneurship – most of us are involved in the environment outside of work. I love this practical implication of science!

We are a bunch of engineers who have fun and like to build things. If you get colleagues interested in the engineering, the science, then you have support. We don't dismiss ideas or change. I believe with such smart people working for the company, if we give them an environmental problem to solve then together we could solve it. People really care, are really passionate about solving a problem – sometimes we will discuss a problem and come up with several solutions just for intellectual interest. This is the type of people we attract. We can make the change – we have somewhere between 80–90,000 employees and hundreds of millions of customers, so when we make a change it has a significant impact.

As a Champion I work on a variety of projects. Within my job I am looking at urban design and development. Extra to this we are looking for ways to make it simple for employees to recycle, and are looking at things in our specific environment – cars, trains, energy, and investing in our local area. I also champion a sustainability mindset; I tell my colleagues that they are too smart to make the wrong decisions when they know what the right ones are.

I am lucky that I'm in the right place at the right time – Microsoft now is seriously investing in the environment, and being in Seattle helps. Also, I live in a democratic nation where there are opportunities to create your dream, make a difference. But I am part of a bigger global grass-roots movement that is very important – if we don't take care of this planet we will die.

Dr Daryl Burnaby, Global Communities Partnership Manager, GlaxoSmithKline (GSK) (UK)

My anchor is my Christian faith and the values my parents taught me. I have worked for GSK since 1999 and was always a sustainability champion. Now with the work Andrew Witty [Chief Executive Officer (CEO)] is doing I am especially proud to be working for GSK.

I have always been a Champion of sustainability, and it is only in this last year that I have become a Specialist. But ever since childhood I have wanted to contribute. I'm not sure if it is my Christian upbringing which shaped my values, or my parents who encouraged me to learn and develop myself and others – or a bit of both. I had a good start in life and always had a thirst for knowledge. This got me into Cambridge University. I was the first in my family to go to university and they encouraged me and were proud of my hard work. It was tough, I had to work things out for myself, but I made good friends. I'm not someone to give up, I'm determined to continue and set myself a high standard and I 'came good'.

I decided to do a PhD to expand the boundaries of my knowledge. I have a thirst for knowledge! I took Environmental Chemistry as it interested me very much. I chose to do the PhD away from family and friends, in Southampton, I think unconsciously to challenge and push myself. During that time I became fascinated in what science can do when applied, how it can help. Because the world is a bit unbalanced it is good to see that science can help me with the question: 'What can I do?' I can use science to bring good to society. I listen to my intuition and decided I could build a career in this. This naturally led me to look at jobs after my PhD in the pharmaceutical sector, which brought me to Glaxo. The motivation to join was definitely personal interest rather than knowing the company.

In 1999 I joined the graduate programme at Glaxo and then moved into Finance there. This gave me a view of GSK from all angles and helped me see the bigger picture. When Glaxo merged with Beecham there was a renewed focus on R&D [research and development] and there was a job opportunity for me to help to shape the direction of that R&D, which I took. I still had my personal passion that the application of science could make a difference, and I liked being part of planning the future of medicines, bringing my skills to the debate. The role pushed me intellectually and I got to see how science really does fit into the bigger picture. The problem is I do get bored easily so I still was looking at other available roles internally. I liked that I had these opportunities to move around and make an impact in different parts of the business.

I gradually became aware of the work that GSK do with community partnerships. Wow! To me this was really exciting, tackling real-world issues and problems, doing projects that made a real societal difference. These were important projects. And I knew that is where I wanted to be. But no roles were available and in the end I waited six years to get the opportunity to join the team. During that time I did champion sustainability and the role that GSK can have in society. I set up projects such as a mentoring programme, which helped me see how I could make an impact, what my unique contribution was. Sometimes when you are part of a big machine you can get lost, but being a mentor helps to see the difference I was making. I could see the benefit for those being mentored but also for employees when given the opportunity to make a difference. A few other staff members joined the initiative; however at the time there was not much active support from GSK for this.

Things became much easier when Andrew Witty became CEO. I can see my thinking is aligned with his, that sustainability and responsibility should be part of how we do business, part of our DNA. He set up Pulse, a programme that encouraged employees to get involved in the community, and that was a real turning point. I wanted to be a part of that. The leadership recognition was really important and gradually things began to change, definitely starting from the top. I would not say that this mindset is embedded across all of GSK, but it is slowly cascading and the organisation has moved on. Our social norms are changing. We do need more infrastructure in place to engage employees, to allow for ideas to be realised and supported as I'm still not sure how I could give an idea the 'legs' it needs to get going.

At times being a Champion was frustrating. I got bogged down in the admin and would lose sight of the bigger picture. I can get disillusioned when I can't see the impact being made. Also, not everyone is aligned to the work, such as middle managers, and this can be frustrating. I'm also nervous about the external environment; where the world is heading. But the work we do, especially in the developing world – it makes me feel 'wow'! We are putting 20% of our Developing Unit profits back into the healthcare infrastructure of Africa, really making a difference. We are doing this because it's the right thing to do, for people and also for our own business in the long term. I am very proud of this, this 'shared value'[3] that we are creating, and when I talk about my work to friends they are wowed by this. I am still worried where humankind are heading, it gets me down a lot as it's not going to be a happy world in the future and the next generation will suffer from this and past generations' actions. How GSK can survive in that is a real challenge. We take one step forward and two steps back. But we are helping things to get worse a bit slower, we are creating pockets of hope.

I now manage a programme where GSK reinvests 20% of the profits generated in the world's least developed countries back into those countries to develop health infrastructure. This typically involves training community health workers to deliver basic healthcare and support material and neonatal health. We have to understand the top health priorities in each of the countries we work in, identifying NGO [non-governmental organisation] partners to deliver the programmes through and developing detailed project plans to deliver the programmes themselves. In the last two years, we have reinvested UK £10 million and set up projects in 34 countries.

I do now feel more proud to be working in the pharma industry, less defensive. I feel more legitimate in what we do. I can see that business can be a force for good, that we have a clear purpose. It has made me more loyal to GSK. For me personally, I realise I need to see the impacts that I create, the result of my work, to motivate me on. I am much clearer now that I do want to make a difference in this world, that we can make a difference at work whilst enjoying my job. And so now I have moved from being a Champion to being a Specialist.

There are three other Champions especially to thank for sharing their time, experiences and insight:

Andrew Brooks is Cocoa Corporate Responsibility andSustainability Manager at Olam in Côte d'Ivoire (Ivory Coast). Born in the UK into a Christian family, Andrew was always interested in languages and specialised in French and Business Administration at university. Attracted to travelling, he entered the cocoa-buying industry and, other than a 15-year period where he worked in London, his career has been focused in the Ivory Coast. Early in his first job post-university at J H Rayner Ltd he engaged with the cocoa and coffee industry in the Ivory Coast, and stayed with the company for over 20 years as it changed hands and name various times. In 1998 he joined Armajaro Trading Ltd, a company that took over the business of dealing with exporters in the Ivory Coast from Phibro and Rayner, and then in 2007 joined Olam because they were keen to invest in Africa – something Andrew strongly believes in. Olam gave him the opportunity to explore different approaches to working with the cocoa industry in the Ivory Coast, and so Andrew introduced a certification programme with Rainforest Alliance to help the farmers improve quality and sustainability of their crops and hence improve their attractiveness to foreign buyers such as Nestlé, Kraft, Cadbury and Mars.

Janice Sloan is Procurement Manager in the UK for Mott MacDonald and a very active Champion of sustainability. Especially close to her mother and grandfather in childhood, they taught Janice the value of challenging herself and taking on responsible roles. She has always been very aware of the impact we have on the planet. As an Army wife Janice travelled around Europe and became a mentor to other Army wives, whilst working for the Civil Service and raising a family. Always determined to stand up for what is right, Janice gets involved in activities that challenge her and make a positive difference, which gives her great job satisfaction. Implementing change at the Civil Service taught her the importance of how people react to change, how working together is important to achieve the whole and the importance of being valued. She joined Mott MacDonald because she saw the role could be challenging and give her the opportunity to make a difference. Janice works closely with the Sustainability team there and promotes good responsible practice. The culture at Mott MacDonald empowers her to develop and get involved and she repays their confidence in her by pushing the boundaries of what they can do to be sustainable. It can be frustrating at times due to lack of time and resources to keep the momentum going, but the work is important and it motivates her that they can make a difference.

Steve Adams is Director of Supply Chain Operations at Coca-Cola Enterprises, UK. Instilled with values of hard work, competitiveness and integrity from his father, Steve felt from childhood the need to make a difference in what he did, to be the best and 'break new ground'. Taking an engineering apprenticeship route so that he could learn from the ground up, Steve worked in the bottling industry (Diageo), first in Engineering and then in Production. In 2000 he joined Coca-Cola Enterprises because of its reputation and the opportunity to work with his boss. At Coca-Cola Enterprises Steve quickly rose through the ranks, and was one of the early engineers who looked at reducing energy in operations and how to operate efficiently and responsibly. Confident he had the skills to make a difference, and with supportive mentors, Steve pushed his boundaries and challenged the status quo around him as he worked his way up in project management, managing capital projects and being a team leader, where he learned that people are the key ingredient for success. Coca-Cola Enterprises has given him opportunities to explore new ways of operating and individual learning, and in the last few years especially has developed a culture that engages and supports employees to be sustainable and entrepreneurial. Steve has turned around failing factories that now win industry awards, and is a prominent Champion for the work he does with their supply chain. He has a passion for sustainability, and loves that Coca-Cola Enterprises' CEO (John Brock) also feels this way. Steve is on the Corporate Responsibility governance structure, is a very active champion, and in his senior role is able to make a real difference to how Coca-Cola Enterprises operates sustainably.

4.2 The corporate Sustainability Champion

Sustainability Champions support and advocate an organisation's approach to being sustainable. They have a job that does not sit within the Sustainability department, thus are not Specialists (although some do aspire to be Specialists and/or work closely with Specialists). Initially, their first interest or passion is usually related to their 'day job' (such as Marketing, Engineer or Sales Consultant) and does not focus specifically on sustainability and responsible business. However, sustainability and/or the opportunity to make a change is important to them and so they take on responsibility extra to their day role in order to create positive impacts.

Champions are change agents and are critical in the process of embedding sustainability into the culture of an organisation. Champions are not initiative- or location-based, although they may be in a physical sense. Rather, they are committed to being part of a strategic change process spreading across the entire organisation and spanning ranks, functions and regions. In practice, many Champions start and have greatest impact in their direct locality, but good Champions form part of a strong network that can influence other departments and locations through company-wide initiatives, communicating stories, enthusing other employees, engaging stakeholders and inspiring other employees to become Champions. Champions are a powerful tool for embedding sustainability into the organisation – from within.

The practical role of a Champion varies depending on the organisation's context, impact, need, resources available and, importantly, the individual

Table 4.1 Example Champion activities

Raise awareness of issues	Run awareness campaigns, sometimes with Communications and Sustainability teams. Communication-based campaigns, or running events, themed days and education programs
Run projects with partners for fundraising (e.g. NGO, charity)	Organising activities or ongoing donations for a specific cause that has been assessed as aligned to corporate agenda and/or staff interests. Often with external partners. Researching options, setting up partnerships, raising awareness and managing the projects
Introduce a change process (i.e. ISO 14000)	Champion a change process, such as certification, joining FTSE4Good, sustainability reporting, or implementing a quality management system such as from the International Organization for Standardization (ISO) or AccountAbility (AA) families. Sometimes works with external advisors
Run projects, sometimes with partners, to change employee behaviour	Working on behaviour change programmes within their specific local, usually with Sustainability Specialists. This could be as campaigns, raising awareness or internal lobbying to introduce recycling options, water conservation in bathrooms or changing cleaning products
Set a good example	Lead by example. Use new certification systems or recycling processes and discuss these with colleagues, show active support. Especially powerful if senior members of the organisation or decision-makers
Run specific projects related to their work	Design, propose and run projects within their job description that are more sustainable than current options. This relates to activities that Social Intrapreneurs do, but Champions tend to run these as projects within their own role rather than rolling them out as separate concerns or divisions

NGO, non-governmental organisation.

Champion's own motivations and style of operating. For example, the time and effort a Champion gives to this work will vary, based on availability, motivation and personal interest. Some – after their initial interest – integrate activities into their day-to-day role such as working on a programme to roll out certification. Others add the work on top of their daily workload, such as being a member of the Green Team and organising Green Weeks or Recycling Drives. Table 4.1 gives examples of activities.

4.3 Understanding the Champion

Although Champions cannot be clustered by gender, age or nationality, there are some clear defining characteristics and it is within their past experiences and upbringing that the foundations exist for why they become Champions later in life. To be a Champion means taking on extra work, being noticed and advocating change – not tasks that guarantee popularity or personal success.[4] Exploring their early-life learned experiences and upbringing helps understand why they do this.

4.3.1 Early learned experiences

Priya (Microsoft) talks about her previous experiences abroad, in India and travelling the world, which gave her a significant appreciation of the interaction between humans and natural resources.

> In India you constantly have to be careful with resources. Travelling in Nepal also showed me how connected we are to the environment and basic resources such as water. In comparison to US, which is a resource-wasteful society, I could see how important environmental resources are for the fulfilment of basic human needs, and for fundamental economic development.

Steve (Coca-Cola Enterprises) talks about influences from his father.

> He was competitive in nature and wanted us to be the best, break new ground. He worked hard and grew his business but at the same time had integrity and was trustworthy. He installed in me the determination to make a difference.

The childhood experiences are not necessarily the same (i.e. the childhood experiences the Champions profiled here vary from travelling experiences to parental influence to political ideology). However, all cite influences in earlier life that have significantly shaped their desires to 'make a difference', 'take responsibility', 'have an impact'.[5] A 2012 US survey of university students and recently employed graduates (at any age) suggests that this is an important factor for many people: 72% of students surveyed wanted a job where they could make an impact, with 52% of employees stating this as well (Net Impact, 2012).

4.3.2 Making a difference

Working hard, or challenging themselves, is also important to Champions. An interest in sustainability could align with this and/or could be a vehicle for Champions to challenge themselves, providing the satisfaction they derive from challenging task completion.

> I like to stretch myself . . . challenge myself, and the status quo!
> (Steve, Coca-Cola Enterprises)

Why do Champions like to be the ones to make a difference? The theory of 'meaning of life' could help explain this. Scientist Viktor Frankl postulated that to understand the meaning of our lives we look for sources that can lead to creating meaning. As discussed earlier, Frankl identified four sources of meaning: through spiritual aspirations, through our deeds (i.e. work), through our experience of values (such as at work) and through our attitudes. For any employee their work (especially through active participation) can be a significant place where meaning can come from; as a source through our deeds (what we do that contributes to the world) and through our experience of values in the workplace. These sources can then reinforce the meaning we give to our lives (Frankl, 1964):

> This is everything I believe in. This is who I am.
>
> (Janice, Mott McDonald)

The research shows that Champions need strong sources of meaning from work and this drives them to be active and work hard in their workplace to make a difference (Bansal, 2003). If their work does not provide enough meaning then they may unconsciously look for or create opportunities, by championing a cause that is personally important to them.

> I waited six years for this opportunity to work here. That is where I want to be, to make a difference.
>
> (Daryl, GSK)

Finding, or creating, this source of meaning through work also gives the Champions opportunities for their values (their ethical ideals) and characteristics (their qualities) to be validated and supported. This validation can further reinforce their 'sense of self': the understanding they have of who they are and their unique place in the world – thus a reinforcing cycle of looking for sources of meaning at work in order to clarify their sense of self, finding it and then being able to enact that source through their deeds, which reinforces that sense of self even further. This cycle can happen if there is congruence between personal and workplace values and characteristics. Active alignment of the personal and organisational values has been seen to reduce dissonance between individuals and the organisation they work for, and also improve sustainability performance (Posner and Schmidt, 1993). Experiencing this reinforcing cycle could be all the more important for Champions as the research showed they have a clear and fixed understanding of who they are as individuals and so a focused set of parameters for what will give meaning to their lives (Amos and Weathington, 2008). Wouter (Reed Elsevier) talks about his desire to help others and as a Champion he has a legitimate platform to do this. Janice (Mott McDonald) talks about wanting to encourage other employees, which Mott McDonald supports her doing in the role of a Champion. Both have found a way to create congruence between personal characteristic and their deeds at work and this then allows them to see that their organisation has attributes similar to their own personal identity, as well as providing opportunities for further self-expression (Collier and Esteban, 2007). This congruence is important for Champions and in turn can self-reinforce their attachment and loyalty to their organisation; all the champions profiled here speak highly of their organisations.[6]

Although our values are usually passive (i.e. not something we focus on every day), they can become non-passive action if the congruence of values between individual and work becomes misaligned, for example, if the status quo at work becomes too different to our individual expectations[7] (Bansal, 2003). Champions are special in that they will more readily move from passive to non-passive action (i.e. champion a cause) to fix that misalignment and make a difference (Bansal, 2003).

> My grandfather always used to say 'Don't settle for the easy road' . . . I will stand up and get involved if it is needed.
>
> (Janice, Mott McDonald)

However, there is always a linear experience that precedes Champions moving from passive to non-passive action:

- A *seed* planted, usually in childhood, which can be values-based (integrity), characteristics-based (confidence) or interest-based (interest in the environment, social justice). Janice (Mott McDonald) talks about having to leave school at 16 in order to earn an income for her family, where she learned early that she had to accept responsibilities.
- An *awakening* moment where this seed was given the opportunity to grow. For example, Priya (Microsoft) talks of her awakening moment during a trip to Nepal where she reflected on the meaning of life.
- The moment of *opportunity*. Andrew (Olam) talks about an instant attraction to Olam when he realised their agendas aligned (investing in Africa) and that they would give him the opportunity to be part of this.

These observations help to explain the motivations behind why Sustainability Champions do what they do; but it is important to acknowledge that they could be examples of a much wider cultural shift.

4.3.3 New social movement

Priya from Microsoft talks about a 'global grassroots' movement spreading across the globe, that she feels part of:

> I'm optimistic, I don't feel alone in this. It is like a grassroots movement but globally. And in the US grassroots movements can make a difference, can be successful. It is part of the American Dream, to be able to create your dream, make the change.

The concept of 'social movement' (Fuchs, 2006, discussed in previous chapters) explains how a society can transform from one phase of accepted norms to the next.[8] I propose that organisations are experiencing this social movement through the emergence of more and more Sustainability Champions as more and more employees – or 'rebels' – are joining. Social Intrapreneurs and Specialists may be active and vocal members of this global sustainability social movement by making it their profession, but Champions are also members – even if probably more unconsciously so, and from within their existing jobs.

In 2011 Saatchi & Saatchi launched the global DOT campaign – Do One Thing. The global campaign asks people to commit to doing at least one thing for a sustainable world – whether at work or home. Some of these actions are small ('use recycled paper'), others larger ('promote sustainability at work', 'focus my company on being more responsible'). As of August 2012 over *32 million* commitments had been logged – Saatchi & Saatchi are aiming for one billion (www.strategyforsustainability.com/do-one-thing/). Prior to the 2012 Rio Earth Summit, the Earth Day Network (which coordinates the yearly Earth Day activities) launched a similar campaign called 'A Billion Acts of Green', where individual global citizens could make an environmentally sustainable pledge as a way to send a clear message to politicians to take the Summit seriously. For example, a pledge to eliminate pesticides and toxic cleaning products was taken by 1,799 individuals and companies. As of August 2012 over *one billion* pledges had been made on the site (http://act.earthday.org/).

It could be that only when most employees globally perform their duties in a responsible and sustainable way – as part of a new social norm – there is a chance of the social, economic and environmental issues being successfully addressed. This will help nudge current society towards the 'tipping point' (Gladwell, 2001) from 'extra' sustainable behaviour towards 'normal' sustainable behaviour; from an unsustainable society to a sustainable one. However, such a tipping point requires all types of Sustainability Champions, all performing equally important but different roles – and the employee Champion type has a critical role in creating and cascading change from within. Many employees may think what they can do is too small to have an impact. However, small actions can make a big difference when combined with lots of other small actions – creating large-scale change.

4.4 Advice for Champions

Being a Sustainability Champion means publically aligning with a cause and taking on commitments above one's expected day job at work. Part of a change programme, the Champion needs to be patient, have perseverance and be forward-thinking. It is not an easy role to take on but for those who do the benefits are opportunities to align personal values with work, be a critical part of creating real change, take on interesting and challenging roles and be noticed at work. If these are your aspirations, and you care about a sustainability-related issue, being a Champion is an effective and realistic way to change the world whilst keeping your day job.

4.4.1 Motivation

It is important that Champions recognise what their motivation is; what they derive meaning from. For example, employees are more likely to have a stronger involvement in sustainability if they have a moral motive (i.e. a moral duty of the organisation to society) instead of a strategic motive (i.e. financial success: Graafland and van de Ven, 2006) and if their self-identity is enhanced through the association with the organisation being sustainable (Whitehouse, 2006).

> We must understand how we should be positioned in society . . . the way we do business, how we create shared value, is important to me.
>
> (Daryl, GSK)

Champions have a personal connection to the issue or activities they take on and are motivated by that. This could be personal to their private lives: Priya (Microsoft) talks about her personal interest in conserving natural resources and in her spare time is cultivating an internal garden for people without outside space at home. Or it could be related to what they do in their work role or the operations of the firm: Wouter (Reed Elsevier) gives examples of other extra work he takes on to make the business more efficient and professional (the Incident Management Team and Business Continuity Team) (Pedersen, 2010).

The issue will often emerge because it is something Champions no longer want to see being disregarded at work. They interpret the issue through the 'lens' they have in their position in the workplace (Cramer *et al.*, 2004)[9] and through the lens of their own values (Hemingway and Maclagan, 2004). If the issue conflicts enough with their expectations, then the issue becomes a 'concern', and a Champion is born.

> I always believed we need to be part of society, create shared value with society. The turning point was when Andrew Witty [CEO] came. He believes this and it is slowly cascading through the organisation. I support that change; we are changing bad habits, I'm championing this shared value.
>
> (Daryl, GSK)

Most Champions focus on that emergent issue, and expand to related activities clustered around that. For example, Steve (Coca-Cola Enterprises) had an initial interest in energy reduction and developed further to address a cluster of related issues such as waste, pollution and ISO 14000 and now supply chain performance – the 'cluster' being environmental issues. Daryl (GSK) has a focus on societal and community issues, initially mentoring in the local community and now overseeing large-scale community investment projects.

It is critical that Champions recognise what the issues are that concern them – that they derive meaning from – as these will motivate them. Taking initiative on issues outside their interest area could potentially motivate less (Hemingway and Maclagan, 2004). It is also important to recognise how they are viewing the issue because of that motivation (a personal lens can alter perception of an issue) and if they have all the facts – an incorrect view that motivates them to unsuitable action could shape how the organisation responds to their championing activities (i.e. in a negative way).

4.4.2 Work style

Each individual has a style of working that fits with their characteristics and the situational context they work in. Finding a style of championing that also fits with the work context is important.

Some Champions are physically positioned in a job where they have resources available to them. Combined with their characteristics, they can initiate direct action in that context:

> I'm not afraid to organise things . . . I organised a 'Walk the Stairs' week. We saw people taking the elevator to go up or even down just one level! So to encourage them to be healthier, and to use less electricity, the Green Team decided to encourage the use of the stairs. So I redesigned the stairs as a piano . . . We linked the week with a diabetes charity we support and people did notice and did use the elevator less. It did help change behaviour, it got people talking and thinking about health and lifestyle issues.
>
> (Wouter, Reed Elsevier)

Other Champions have a different style of working because their context is different (such as fewer resources), have different personal characteristics and work in cultures where more subtle action is needed:

> I had lack of time and resource, and not enough central recognition or promotion. So I talk about concepts as the right way of doing business – as good, responsible business practices. I work one on one with people to help them understand the fundamental approach to being sustainable, and show them through practical examples such as certification or integrated quality management systems. I keep chipping away.
>
> (Janice, Mott McDonald)

Finding the style – relative to characteristics, work situation and corporate culture – is a great enabler. The context should not be an excuse to limit Champions, rather to help them understand *how* they can best make change and clarify what support they need from their line manager, organisation processes, other champions and the Sustainability team. For example, Janice has the positional authority to talk to high-ranking people but lacks the time to run many full-scale initiatives. A group of Champions supporting her, who have time to run initiatives but not the positional power to get them approved (which she can do), could be mutually supportive and highly effective.

4.4.3 Tactics of a change agent

The tactics of a 'change agent' are very useful for Champions to learn. A change agent is someone in the organisation introducing and embedding change – regardless of what that actual change is. This is clearly similar to what Sustainability Champions do and utilising their skills to create sustainability-related change can be very successful. Key change agent skills include:

- Connecting conversations to what is perceived to be on the organisational agenda – i.e. that which is perceived to be relevant to the organisation and therefore employees have 'permission' to address. The unspoken politics of an organisation can often be the driving force for what gets done, so understanding how the politics work is important. Issues identified not as threats, rather as opportunities that can be resolved, are often more likely to be supported by top management than irresolvable issues (Butcher and Clarke, 2001).
- If an issue is not currently clearly connected to something on the organisational agenda then it can help instead to link it directly to the espoused values of the organisation. As discussed previously, the values of the organisation (and how they manifest in practice) can strongly influence employee perception of the organisation and why they want to be connected to that organisation (Bansal, 2003).
- Communicating what Champions do and why, so that those they work with are aware, can inspire others. However, it is important not to become the office bore as there is a fine line between informing and 'dictating'. Sharing your passion and success stories can be inspiring, but lecturing on what a fellow employee is doing wrong can be negative and off-putting. It is also important not to become the 'conscience' of the group where activities can be outsourced to the Champion; communicating opportunities and inviting others to participate or learn more is a way of addressing that risk.
- Seeking out other Sustainability Champions and connecting with them does help. The Sustainability Specialists should help with this connection so that Champions can share tactics and success stories, give each other

advice and get encouragement from the fact that others in the organisation care about similar issues. There is also power in numbers!

- It is critical to have senior line management support, or the support of senior members of the organisation. They can legitimise what a Champion does, and in some instances give them resources, time and authority to run certain initiatives. If line or senior management support needs to be developed, investing time in doing this can reap big rewards later when support is needed. A Champion needs to seek approval via either the legitimate systems of power used in the organisation (e.g. formal sign-off) or the informal (shadow) systems used (those with influence, the gate-keepers) (Houchin and Maclean, 2005).

4.4.4 Engaging middle managers (the 'black hole')

The phrase 'But what has this got to do with me?' is one often heard by Champions from co-workers. The perception can exist within middle management that being sustainable is the responsibility of the board, top management, the Specialists, Champions . . . but not them. Middle management employees are less likely to take on ownership the way Champions such as Janice (Mott McDonald) and Steve (Coca-Cola Enterprises) do as they expect those with authority or specific responsibility to take the necessary action; those other employees who have a broader view of the business, leadership responsibilities, and may understand better the multiple pressures in the macro environment. Often front-line staff may also understand these pressures because of their proximity to external stakeholders and therefore have a better view of societal and environmental pressures and be more ready to take action to create a sustainable organisation. However, those employees not as exposed to the external environment are less able to see the need to be sustainable. They often face operational-based challenges such as cost-cutting or pressure of sales targets and find it hard to see how to reconcile these with being a responsible and sustainable business. This is called 'the middle management black hole' (Grayson, 2008).

However, an organisation will find it very hard to be truly sustainable until all employees have a sustainable mindset – until sustainability is embedded into mindset and culture. Chapter 1 (Unsung Heroes) addresses this at an organisational level. Champions can take specific actions to help their colleagues who may not have the stakeholder view they enjoy, or the confidence, knowledge or initiative. Champions can look for specific opportunities where other employees can engage with the issues in a constructive way that creates outcomes – seeing that activities have an outcome can motivate others to get involved. For example, Wouter (Reed Elsevier) talks of his 'Walk the Stairs' week: in this example a Champion could recruit a member from each relevant department to take part in the campaign and follow up afterwards to their colleagues with information on how much electricity and CO2 emissions were saved in that week, extrapolated to a year and then on a personal level how many trees a single person could save in a year just by walking the stairs.

Using the power of the informal, verbal story-telling information system of the organisation can be a powerful tactic as well (Cramer *et al.*, 2004). Champions can share what the CEO and other influential members say about sustainability in conversations to colleagues, which can spread on the organisation's 'grapevine'.[10] Finding and sharing specific activities/campaigns/ targets met/positive results ('symbolic acts') from around the organisation can give clarity to the work, and sharing them with fellow employees can motivate others to get involved (Bansal, 2003). If a direct colleague or line manager is not interested, other senior members might be supportive – they could become a mentor, giving advice on how to work within the politics of the organisation and share stories with their immediate colleagues. Sometimes, finding the clear 'wins' (such as awards, positive press coverage) and communicating them internally can give clarity to how a big concept like sustainability is relevant to the organisation (Washington and Hacker, 2005).

> You need to help the individual understand why this is good for them.
>
> (Janice, Mott McDonald)

Understanding how to talk with people is also important for engaging middle management, for example, using language and themes as a way of capturing their attention and creating meaning specifically for them, in their context and with the view they have because of where they are physically positioned in the organisation (Whitehouse, 2006). Meaning can be created through social interaction such as conversations, for example talking about specific issues related to their work rather than focusing on abstract high-level concepts (Bansal, 2003). Help them to construct meaning in their context relative to their motivations and work situation, and develop and be consistent with language as that can create clarity and familiarity. This requires looking at the issue through their lens and using language (specific words, conversational tone, the relevant examples to use) they can construct meaning from (Cramer *et al.*, 2004).

4.5 Advice for organisations

Champions tend to be loyal and hard-working, and many are already respected within the organisation. They are valuable employees to have, and it is important for managers and Human Resources (HR) to understand that their motivation is to make the organisation better and therefore it is worth nurturing them. More and more Sustainability Specialists and HR specialists realise the value of Champions and create a system for both organising the work Champions do and for supporting them – such as a network.

4.5.1 Building a network or community

Many Champions have emerged through their own initiative to address issues they believe their organisation is not addressing responsibly:

> A community of practice where groups of people come together who share a concern, set of problems or a passion about a topic, and who deepen their knowledge and expertise in this area . . . they don't necessarily work together every day, but they meet because the find value in their interactions.
>
> (Wenger *et al.*, 2002)

These 'communities' can be naturally self-organising, or organised by the Sustainability Specialists. They can be platforms for emergent creativity and knowledge – 'Engines for the development of social capital' (Lesser and Storck, 2001).

> Together we do push the boundaries. We think a bit differently and are challenging the status quo. If something is being done because that is the way it has always been done – but I see it misaligned with how we should do business or societal need – I ask why. Champions make a difference, and this excites me.
>
> (Steve, Coca-Cola Enterprises)

These networks or communities are currently becoming more structured and planned, usually by the Sustainability Specialists. A Champions network can a formal or informal structure that can be used to organise Champion activity, a way for the Sustainability Specialists to support them and bring clarity to their role, to enable them to have impact and ensure distribution of resources. The type of structure for the network works best when it is relative to the organisational culture and the objectives of the network, and so should be developed with the organisational culture in mind. It is worth considering (Exter, 2009) that:

- A network can be formal, or explicit, with a clear leader, levels (usually by rank) and clear roles and expectations. This helps with organisation and gathering information. However in some organisational cultures this formal approach can stifle creativity and reduce the discretion that Champions have for experimentation.
- An informal or implicit network is flexible enough to deal with expansion or contraction/churn, and allow some interpretation to be relevant at a local level, especially in global organisations. However, an informal network can sometimes inhibit communication and sharing of resources and best practice between Champions because they don't have a clear avenue for talking with each other or dedicated resources for knowledge sharing.

The size of a network also varies, depending on the size of the company, geographical spread and stage the organisation is at for embedding (i.e. if starting, there may only initially be a few Champions because recruitment has not yet started).

A successful network is usually planned at least to some degree (whether formally recognised or not), initiated and managed by the Sustainability Specialists. It is critical that the Sustainability Specialists manage the network and Champions in a professional way. A well-planned network needs a clear leader Champion such as the CEO; teams grouped around themes; and organisational impacts/targets (i.e. environment, workplace practices). Common tools are creating a dedicated section on an existing intranet, bespoke training, relevant conferences, weekly emails or newsletters, a portal for suggestions of ideas and planned engagement tactics to keep Champions motivated. These all contribute to the success of a Champions network.

4.5.2 Supporting a Champion

The Sustainability Specialist has a key role in supporting Champions, as do those employees who line-manage Champions. Although having a group of employees asking difficult questions or asking for extra resource to (e.g.) recycle can at first seem disruptive, their actions are positive for the company and should be encouraged. As explored earlier, if supported they can become very loyal employees. They can enable the organisation towards targets, be a source of innovation and solve problems because of their different way of thinking. Support from the CEO and line managers is therefore a legitimate request and will also be a key enabler for Champions.

> That John Brock is passionate about being a sustainable business does without doubt make a huge difference.
>
> (Steve, Coca-Cola Enterprises)

Further, for some (such as Daryl, GSK), a CEO who actively promotes sustainable practices can be the 'permission' they need to become a more active Champion. Sustainability Specialists and organisational leaders should work together to communicate the importance placed on sustainability; that sustainability is firmly on the corporate agenda and employees have permission to engage intellectually.

However, Champions need to be part of a wider, coordinated effort across the organisation that is being championed by members of the extended leadership team. For initiatives to have real impact there needs to be a connection to the formal and explicit organisational agenda and objectives (Bansal, 2003). When legitimate organisational leaders are clear about what impacts are being addressed, why (i.e. because of new data, legislation or a rise in stakeholder priorities) and how the impacts can be addressed, then Champions are usually better accepted as relevant to the business.

Sustainability Specialists can also be clear on what support they specifically can put in place to support Champions, whether a way to share ideas for projects, help get permissions for initiatives, find other Champions to help organise activities or provide specific research on the business case for being sustainable relevant to the Champion's position in the organisation. Some Sustainability Specialists organise live chats and toolkits, and share success stories via internal communication platforms. Others provide global initiatives, such as a competition, and advice for Champions on how to run them locally. In turn, some Champions in global organisations act as the local contact point for Specialists, helping them with access to relevant managers for global roll-out of (for example) a measurement and reporting process (Exter, 2009).

As Champions tend to be passionate about a specific area (such as environment or community engagement) they could be demotivated if their specific initiative is not addressed. Not all issues relevant to sustainable business can be addressed at once, and the Sustainability Specialists will have helped the organisation to set priorities and targets and a route to achieving those targets. Communicating this plan – and the reasons behind it – to Champions is therefore important. Further, it can help to show Champions when their concern will be addressed and what they can do meanwhile. Showing them the impact of their work also helps.

> It is extremely important to see the impact of what we do. For me personally, and for other employees in the business.
>
> (Daryl, GSK)

The culture of an organisation is also an enabler or barrier for Champions, and understanding this is important and worth having discussions with either HR (if they view the culture of an organisation as an asset to be developed) or a colleague who has a good understanding of the culture and how to get things done. 'Culture' refers to why things get done (motivation) and how things get done (such processes and procedures) – together equalling 'the way things get done around here' (Deal and Kennedy, 1982). A good culture can motivate Champions, support and nurture them. It can likewise contribute to economic success (Barclay, 2010). A negative culture can do the opposite. Recognising this and working initially within parameters of that culture is critical (see Chapter 1, Unsung Heroes, for more on this).[11]

> When it gets tough I keep chipping away. Because the culture here is that it will happen, someone will hear and that motivates me.
>
> (Janice, Mott McDonald)

Line managers of Champions can enable their work as well. As discussed earlier, supporting the passion that Champions have can enable them in positive action for the organisation and also reinforce their loyalty to the organisation. Therefore, on a practical level it can help if line managers also allow Champions a high degree of individual discretion in their Championing activities so that Champions can reflect, assess and make decisions based on correct facts, understand their motivation and have the 'space' to think of innovative solutions. Managers' individual discretion is important in improving sustainability performance (Swanson, 1995) as it allows Champions to explore why they are taking action, what they hope to achieve, set goals and apply discretionary behaviour extra to their day job. Further, their commitment to the cause they are championing can encourage discretionary behaviour, and so stifling this can discourage that discretionary behaviour to take action (Collier and Esteban, 2007). Sustainability Specialists and HR professionals can negotiate this 'space' with a Champion's line manager.

> I am given the freedom and discretion to work outside the usual parameters. I'm trusted, even expected, to get on and do it.
>
> (Janice, Mott McDonald)

Finally, recognising the work of Champions is important, both to share what they do with others and also to recognise and validate their hard work.

> I did not know I was recognised, that is nice that people noticed. People taking seriously what I do.
>
> (Wouter, Reed Elsevier)

> It has helped to see the confidence that my managers have in me.
>
> (Andrew, Olam)

4.6 Concluding thoughts

In 2009 I wrote a 'how to' guide for Specialists giving advice on developing Champions and a Champions network (Exter, 2009). In 2009 it was the only publicly available guide we could find giving advice on Sustainability Champions, but in the intervening time more and more companies are utilising Champions and talking about them as part of how they both engage employees and their approach to embedding sustainability. Today, it is therefore much easier to find examples of Sustainability Champions and Specialists working together. For individuals, being a Champion can be a powerful platform for expression of who they are, how they can live their values at work and how they can connect better with their organisation. Therefore, from the individual and organisational perspective, Champions are a critical asset in the drive to be sustainable. Being a Sustainability Champion is a tangible way that any employee can change the world while keeping their day job.

4.6.1 Summary advice

- Recognise your personal interest and motivation for becoming a Champion as this can help you identify your strengths and weaknesses.
- Understand what is driving you to take action, as this can help set the parameters for what you will and will not want to do.
- Negotiate with your line manager about your Champion work, for discretion and support. This can be through presenting a business case, showing how it advances your work and personal development, or by utilising the credibility or moral authority you have.
- Contact the Sustainability Specialists in your organisation and share your interest, what you want to do, and find out what platforms they have to support you.
- Understand the culture of your organisation – the legitimate and shadow systems – so that you can strategically choose change tactics that will work in your context.
- Explore the skills of a change agent, such as crafting language, understanding how to engage others and how to use organisational agenda or values to legitimise your work
- Seek out other Sustainability Champions, whether in a network or informally, and share best practice, ideas and advice.
- Be strong and confident and believe in what you are doing!

4.7 Further reading

Deal TE, Kennedy AA (1982). *Corporate Cultures*. Reading, MA: Addison-Wesley.

Drennan D (1992). *Transforming Company Culture*. London: McGraw-Hill.

Exter N (2009). *How to Build a Corporate Responsibility Champions Network*. Cranfield: Cranfield University.

Exter N (2011). *How to Engage Employees in Corporate Responsibility*. Cranfield: Cranfield University.

Porter M, Kramer M (2011). Creating shared value. *Harvard Business Review* 89 (1/2): 62–77.

Posner BZ, Schmidt WH (1993). Values congruence and differences between the interplay of personal and organizational value systems. *Journal of Business Ethics* 12 (5): 341–347.

Schein E (2006). *Career Anchors*. San Francisco: Wiley.

Visser W (2008). *Making A Difference: Purpose-Inspired Leadership for Corporate Sustainability and Responsibility (CSR)*. Saarbrücken: VDM.

5 The Sustainability Godparent

Godparent: (noun) an experienced employee who acts as an advisor and guide to a junior or other member of staff; (verb) providing support, feedback, advice, training and taking specific action to enable another employee in their work.

Mentors are well known in business, (usually) senior employees who give support, guidance and advice to a more junior member of staff (the protégé). This support can be formal or informal. However, there is a type of employee who goes beyond mentoring; they help and advise the protégé to navigate the organisation as a political entity and critically they take specific actions and interventions to enable their protégés in their work. This is a Godparent. Some Sustainability Godparents have a specific focus or interest in sustainability as a specialist subject; others do not but trust their protégé in his or her interest in sustainability.

Sustainability Godparents are hard to find as individuals; however most Specialists, Champions, Unsung Heroes and Social Intrapreneurs give credit to a more senior employee who helped them to navigate the political structures of their organisations to get their ideas and projects to launch. Godparents tend to work within close proximity (placement in organisation or physical proximity) to the protégé. A Head of Sustainability – although a Specialist – can be a Godparent, as can a Senior Champion. The roles are not mutually exclusive, although there are many instances where the Godparent does not work within sustainability; rather the Godparent is a line manager or human resources (HR) professional.

The first part of this chapter shares two examples of Sustainability Godparents, with a glimpse into their motivations and detail on what they did as Godparents. The second part of the chapter briefly explores what could motivate a middle or senior manager to be a Godparent, and further highlights what potential Godparents can do – the toolkit of skills and actions to use. Godparents care, whether about their protégés or also about sustainability and the organisation. Anyone can be a Godparent, if not suited to be a Champion, Specialist, Social Intrapreneur or Unsung Hero. But it is clear that

Sustainability Godparents are a critical enabler of the success that others achieve – and take on this role as part of their day job.

5.1 Case studies

Justin Evans, Leader, UK-Middle East and Africa Social Infrastructure Market, Arup (UK)[1]

Godparent to Jo da Silva[2]

> *My role? I persuaded the board I should take an interest in her . . . Have you met Jo? She is a maverick! The system has difficulty handling them . . . I gave her space. I facilitated all that – her natural entrepreneurial side.*

I'm a Structural Engineer, and did a degree in civil engineering with architecture and a post-grad degree at Imperial (UK), in engineering. Arup is the second company I've worked for. I think I am sensitised to sustainability, going back to some work I was doing when the Brundtland Report was published [in 1987]; I was at a UN [United Nations] summer school, at Stansted airport as I recall, as a student. At the time we had a think tank in Arup and I was a young guy invited on to it and presented the conclusions of the Brundtland Report to them. So that was the beginning of my awareness of the One Planet sustainability agenda. This is not unusual in Arup – it is a forward-thinking type of organisation. We do a lot of sustainable consulting work and have a lot of sustainability activists.

Jo and I crossed paths when she was younger; she worked for me as a new graduate engineer out of Cambridge. Over time I maintained a link to Jo through the Arup broader network. When she came back from her work in Sri Lanka after the tsunami, she was keen to establish a group doing things to alleviate poverty but also engage in the broader sustainability agenda, particularly in the developing world.

I would say that I've actively been her sponsor for 18 months. It started with a couple of chance conversations – Jo was finding it difficult to make her great idea happen and there was a lot of organisational 'treacle' that prevented her getting off the starting blocks effectively. I would say my role was, well . . . I persuaded the board I should take an active interest in her and the international development business and reassured them that we could make it work.

At the time the two sections of the business had become a bit intertwined: International Development and Arup Cause. Philanthropic activities are channelled through Arup Cause, which is quite central to the beliefs and values of the firm and an aspect of our social responsibility. At a high level, we believe we need to actively give back to society. That spans a whole series of activities – separate discussions. But we also did a lot of international development work. The link between our international development work and philanthropic cause work – well, Jo was in the middle of that.

I helped her establish international development, ring fencing it, and set it up as a non-profit business within the firm with a different business model and overhead structure. Jo and her fledgling international development team at that time was part of the consulting bit of Arup at the time and she was struggling with too high overheads and the investment of people who didn't really understand her business. My role was to open some white space – so, for example, we transferred her responsibilities for Arup Cause on to other people. I could help her articulate a new vision for a new type of business in the firm – and make that non-threatening. The non-profit thing in our organisation is a bit of a step but an important step if we are going to make a difference in that field.

I was keen to get the right business model which properly chimes with the international development community. We could provide them (NGOs [non-governmental organisations] and a series of other organisations from the UN to International Federation of Red Cross, Rockefeller Foundation and so on) with access to Arup's expertise and specific services on disaster risk reduction, poverty alleviation. Rather than trying to do it as part of our normal business, Jo and I developed a new model for the way that business should operate. For example, we created devoted decision-making, a short reporting line directly into the board, and limited overheads to only those that are relevant to the operation of ArupID [Arup International Development]. ArupID has a high degree of autonomy within a very clear business mission and is a non-profit with a reduced set of overheads. It is given space in the global Arup world to address international development projects with clients – in South Asia, Central and South America. And so Jo and her team were transferred across to ArupID.

I gave her space. I simply facilitated her natural entrepreneurial side.

You have to understand our background, the impact of our founder Ove Arup. His legacy lives on powerfully because of his beliefs and values, because of his fundamental philosophy, which is our legacy, his gift to us. I was fortunate enough to meet him but Jo and others haven't. But he was so prolific in his writings; it's still very much part of the firm. His key speech, although it was written over four decades ago, it still has currency and helps people understand Arup and why we do what we do. It's why we try to weave sustainability into the everyday work we do and influence our clients to adopt principles of sustainable development. It's reasonably successful – so we have a strong thread of sustainability that derives from our interest in the environment, low carbon, climate change and innovation generally. Sustainability policy underpins a lot of these things and allows me to articulate work Jo is doing. So why do we do all these things? We want to be the best in our field, want to apply these things to make the world a better place for people.

Innovation is something that challenges us regularly. We are trying to keep ahead of the field; trying to create a culture of innovation and mobilise all of staff to challenge orthodoxy, the status quo. How do we mobilise the energy innovation talents of our people to produce solutions that others can't? And address the needs of our clients and the world in general? We try to do it in a lot of different ways. For example, we can reapply what we've gained in that same area with a different team in another part of the firm through Arup Projects and the Skills Network. This works well in Arup because of this collective identity; there is a culture of sharing in the firm – in some sense that is derived from the fact we are co-owners. So if I help Shiguru in Tokyo (Head of Arup Japan), I benefit from that because if he does a good job, I benefit. It's that willingness to share and the systems to enable the flow of information and knowledge around the firm. It is difficult – but important – to achieve.

The 'treacle' thing though – that is a lot to do with people not understanding, not taking the time to understand. We like to think at Arup we are an innovative organisation and encourage a culture of innovation. But in terms of the management of projects, delivery of the bottom line – the day-to-day weave and weft of a business . . . for mavericks, although conceptually they are celebrated, the system has difficulty handling them.

I think it did take some effort . . . but Arup is a reasonably fertile ground for these things to take hold.

Cassiano Mecchi, previously HR Manager at Danone, Brazil, now Talent Scout at Google (Latin America)

Godparent to Lucas Urbano[3]

> *I am the HR guy. I had a personal agenda with sustainability . . . secretly I put sustainability in the selection criteria . . . Lucas was rare . . . we created a 'Frankenstein-like' structure for him! The biggest legacy is the change in the mindset.*

I joined Danone already with a personal agenda with a sustainability proposal. I came in via the trainee programme and within the cohort of 23; I was the only one coming from the third sector. This was in 2006. I joined Human Resources (HR) – an area which, in most organisations, is far away from sustainability but HR is strategic at Danone as they fight for talent. In my role I perceived that I had a great potential to select people with the right attitude. The company was growing; it had virtually doubled in size by the time I left in 2010. My main activity was recruiting. So I entered with the aim of identifying people from the outside who could help us to see sustainability as well as people interested in the topic already inside [Danone]. Where are the potential allies inside and outside? So secretly I put sustainability in the selection criteria which appeared in my talks.

After two years I was working more in the corporate area and I was in charge of internships and trainee programmes. I saw that there were a lot of 'tree huggers' who don't know the business. On the other side there were business people who never thought about sustainability because they were never challenged to do so. This is now changing; many candidates see this as something which can be blended. And then there were some hidden gems who thought it ought to be integrated and had some ideas on how to do it. These are rare.

It is great to work on the trainee programme with the top candidates which come in with a great potential. It was also great as several things happened at the same time: the same year a new guideline was issued by headquarters which took socio-environmental aspects seriously. Socio-environmental criteria were made part of the variable payment of executive directors; suddenly the board saw they were responsible for CO_2 emissions. So the moment this happened they implemented these indicators for their teams and it trickled down the hierarchy. This had a strong impact and changed quite a lot in the organisation. And it was not philanthropy; it made sense to the business.

So I already had established myself as the change agent and was involved in sustainability initiatives. And I asked myself what a career development path for a professional in sustainability would look like, what competences this person needs. But there was nothing. I was aware that I could help and all of a sudden I was the person officially at HR who was in charge of sustainability [recruitment and training].

Danone wanted to structure a new area for sustainability but we had little budget. So my idea was to start with a trainee and an intern – to keep it cheap and keep sourcing and selecting under my expertise. The sponsor was the Vice President for R&D [research and development] and Innovation. In 2008 we opened these two jobs. I need to confess that I was too optimistic about finding the right people; we had a lot of candidates that were either 'tree-huggers' or hard-core business people but no one understanding both worlds. But in one of the last assessment groups Lucas showed up.

He did very well in the selection process and got inspired when he heard that there was a position in sustainability. He entered as trainee. He had an aggressive development plan that meant within two years he would enter a management position. Lucas was a rare exception because he did not only succeed in the normal selection process; he also had the sustainability background and an entrepreneurial spirit that were essential for creating a new area. So what I said to him was: 'this is a great challenge, you will get a lot of resistance, but I trust you.'

Now I see that it was [meant to be] him; but then it was a gamble.

The development plan for trainees is very aggressive. However, it was part of my Machiavellian plan to help sustainability grow quickly by using the trainee programme which had the purpose of rapid growth. And we had aggressive objectives for environmental and social objectives coming from the headquarters in France. So the Executive Committee took the sponsorship and especially the Vice President for R&D and Innovation who was trained in this area. So she had a legitimate interest and she was up for developing the area and helping with the cause. However, the distance between her as director and Lucas the trainee was too big. She could not take care of him 100%. So we created a 'Frankenstein-like' structure so that Lucas reports to a supply chain manager who was also a top talent within the organisation with good evaluations and potential. The guy was a good supervisor and people manager, but lacked the view on sustainability – he had more the 'whatever' attitude. By pairing him up with Lucas, they taught each other what they knew best and things moved even faster.

So it took someone above Lucas who knew how to play chess and took care to put the right pieces together; it was very wise to set up this structure for Lucas to grow.

The biggest insight he had was him talking to other areas of the business with the understanding of how he could contribute. Walmart is very relevant as a client and they started to introduce sustainability in purchasing. So if a key client was asking for it and Lucas came in saying, your key client is asking for sustainability and you don't know how to do it – I can help . . . this got him heard.

I am the HR guy. So in my opinion the biggest legacy is the change in the mindset. Agreeing or not, interested or not – every employee at Danone was impacted by sustainability. I had many talks with, for example, sales people who said that their children are aware of recycling and they can now tell them that their employer is doing something. So the objectives which came from France turned into a more holistic understanding. Now all the employees understand sustainability and think twice before they adopt something in their job.

In my current job I can identify many Intrapreneurs. So within my role in HR I always think about how I can help this talent flourish in order to have a positive social and/or environmental impact. In Latin America I see now more and more candidates with this profile. There are some real interesting talents mixing business and sustainability. What makes my eyes shine is if the person brings this spontaneously; someone thinking how to incorporate social or environmental factors into existing projects. If, for instance, there is a project aiming at small and medium businesses and one candidate says: 'Why don't we target NGOs as well?', that is a plus in the selection process. If this person later joins the company and no one has an answer to that question, they may have the opportunity to go on, design this process, implement it, and leverage the impact the company has – in a natural manner, without having to be forced into it.

Note: *Cassiano's story is from his time at Danone. He now works for Google as a Talent Scout.*

5.2 The Sustainability Godparent

It is often said that middle management is a true danger area in organisations – a 'black hole' where ideas, initiatives and good intentions can be swallowed up and disappear. This could be because some middle managers can get 'lost' in the hierarchy of an organisation and become disengaged, apathetic and resentful – or simply do not have the time, resource, motivation or interest to get involved (Grayson, 2008). However, there is a type of change-making middle-management employee who can help to make a difference quite easily. They are keen to share their knowledge, skills and power and have the ability to take small actions that have powerful consequences. Specifically for sustainability, these employees help Champions, Social Intrapreneurs, Specialists and Unsung Heroes in their purpose and actions. They are Sustainability Godparents and are engaged, proactive, motivated, occasionally maverick – and change-makers. They enable others to be successful and have valuable experience, skills, political know-how, power and seniority to help; they are often mentioned as why a Social Intrapreneur, Champion or Specialist finds the way to be successful. The Sustainability Godparent is a role any middle- or senior-level manager can take on – and benefit from – if they feel the other roles profiled in this book are not suitable for them.

Although research on Sustainability Godparents is still very new and only recently emerging, among the Godparents researched most are positioned within traditional departments such as HR, Supply Chain or R&D. Only a few are senior members of the Sustainability team, or sit within the Chief Executive Officer (CEO) office and have a responsibility for driving sustainability through the organisation. All, however, have an awareness of sustainability-related issues such as climate change, resource scarcity or poverty in communities – if even from a distance or only with a general awareness. Those with a passion for sustainable business proactively work to create an internal network of other employees interested and take on the role of Godparent to one or more of these employees. Others become Godparents because they trust and respect a subservient member of their team who is championing sustainability, and engage with that individual because of that personal connection.

A Godparent is similar to a mentor – a more familiar role in business – with similar motivations, benefits and outcomes. What mentors give is quite specific, however: career development, role model and psychosocial support (wisdom and reasoning ability: Sosik and Lee, 2002). Godparents do mentor but in addition to this they take specific interventionist actions typically outside the parameters of a mentor–protégé relationship (Table 5.1).

5.3 Understanding the Godparent

As a very newly identified type of sustainability change-maker, less is known about the Sustainability Godparent than the other types of change-makers. The literature is clear that mentors are motivated to support other employees for a multitude of reasons: some are assigned protégés as part of an organisational system of mentoring; some take on mentoring because of a personal connection or relationship with the protégé; others find satisfaction in enabling others; and some enjoy the status being a mentor can bring (Scandura *et al.*, 1996). However, when considering Godparents – such as Cassiano and Justin, profiled here, but also considering the Champion Janice (Mott McDonald), profiled in Chapter 4, who could also be described as a Godparent– they are both Sustainability Champions and Godparents. Their

Table 5.1 Actions of a Sustainability Godparent

Basic mentoring-related actions of a Godparent	Additional Godparent-based actions
Sharing information that may not be available to the protégé	Two-way process of influence
Teaching job-related skills, whether 'soft skills', such as networking, or technical skills related to the job role	Collaborative working relationship
Network on behalf of the protégé for a narrow range of benefits, such as career advancement	Specific interventionist action, such as finding funding or sponsorship for a project, positioning the protégé in a place of opportunity, or creating new organisational systems for the protégé in order for the protégé's innovations to be realised
Shape motivation by introducing the protégé to a different opinion, way of thinking or challenging the protégé intellectually	Active lobbying by the Godparent for the protégé's mission/project
Confidence building for both mentor and protégé	Engage with and influence decision-makers that the protégé would not have access to
Introduce protégés to decision-makers they otherwise would not have access to	If line manager/senior enough, give protégés discretion in their role, and the 'space' to experiment and develop proposals. For example, with dedicated time for projects, reducing performance goals or incorporating the change-making tasks into the protégé's job description
Advise how to navigate the political structures of the organisation	Benefits for the Godparent: rejuvenate interests and motivations; create a unique identity or status in the organisation; build confidence to guide others; give unique access to different perspectives
Be a 'sounding board', a critical friend	Lend power or authority to the protégé
	Trust the protégé

motivation is directly related to their passion for corporate sustainability and also a joy of seeing others learn, grow in confidence and succeed.

> Recognising social, economic and environmental impacts we're part of – we're about delivering practical solutions that address the needs of the day . . . 'The changing needs of the world' is an easy phrase – but each generation has massive issues to deal with.
>
> (Justin, Arup)

I entered Danone already with a personal agenda with a sustainable proposal . . . So after two to three years in the company I already had established myself as the change agent and was involved in sustainability initiatives.

(Cassiano, when at Danone)

However, Cassiano further has a professional interest in developing employees, as an HR professional. He has a personal passion for sustainable business and being a Sustainability Godparent allows him to bring together his desires to mentor and enable others with his passion for sustainable business:

In my role I perceived that I had a great potential to select people with the right attitude . . . Great potential to work on the trainee programme with the top candidates which come in with great potential.

The role of a Sustainability Godparent can be formal or informal; formally, it may be part of a mentoring programme initiated by HR or the Sustainability team that develops further into a Godparent role. The role can also be informal, working 'under the radar' – as seen with Cassiano when at Danone. However, spontaneous mentoring tends not to be as successful as mentoring done via a programme or platform (Scandura *et al.*, 1996), often because informal mentoring does not set clear boundaries and expectations for mentor and protégé. But because of the determination of Godparents such as Justin and Cassiano to enable their protégés to make real change, this could be less of an issue for Sustainability Godparents; the case studies show a determination actively to acknowledge, plan, and execute their role; and set clear parameters for the relationship.

5.3.1 Benefits of being a Godparent

Why should middle managers be open to the idea of becoming a Sustainability Godparent? Many of the roles profiled in this book may not be suitable for all; the very nature of these roles is that extraordinary action is needed. The learned experiences, motivations and skills of the individual are perhaps more representative of the future societal norms we are shifting towards (i.e. new social movement theory and the Sustainability Movement: see Introduction for more on this) but are not yet at. For the mass of employees whose motivation does not primarily arise from creating change or who do not seek to attain significant meaning for their life from their workplace, the role of Godparent could work well. A Godparent can provide other sources of meaning for an individual, such as:

- Strengthen their individual legitimacy in the workplace because of the unique and valuable knowledge they can share with a few other employees. The term 'Kingmaker' has been used to describe the employee with the power 'behind the throne' who, through the sharing of expertise and experience, enables the worthy of success (Scandura *et al.*, 1996).

- Being a Godparent (and mentor) can give confidence that the knowledge of how to work in the organisational culture is valuable and a critical asset.
- Being paired with an enthusiastic employee with a different way of thinking can rejuvenate Godparents and introduce them to new interesting perspectives and opinions, from which the Godparent can learn technical or industry-related aspects that make them better at their job (Ragins and Scandura, 1999).
- Godparents can expand their network inside the organisation, especially with newer employees who may be on a 'fast-track' route to management; as Lucas was in Danone.
- With intergenerational mentoring or Godparenting, personal satisfaction can arise from the knowledge and evidence of fostering the development of a young adult (Ragins and Scandura, 1999).

5.3.2 Dynamic Duos

Intergenerational Godparenting (when a younger protégé is paired with an older or more senior member of staff) is an area of research being explored by a coalition of academia, business and not-for-profit. Called the Second Half programme,[4] they define this intergenerational collaboration as 'Dynamic Duos'. Their research focuses on demographic change specific to the ageing population – and particularly intergenerational tensions – and what this means for business action and policy-making. Among the emerging solutions to intergenerational tensions, they are exploring this new business archetype, the Dynamic Duos, as an advanced form of mentoring:

> Dynamic Duo: Moving well beyond traditional mentoring, dynamic duos are inter-generational (and often cross-disciplinary) collaborations operating top-down and bottom-up, outside-in and inside-out, to the benefit of both partners – while driving innovation and creating significant new value for their organisations.
>
> (Second Half, 2010)

The research team argue that Dynamic Duos can be a fundamental intergenerational building block, joint working between the baby boomers (and older generations) and those coming up behind to bridge the generations. As with Godparents, instead of the learning being largely one-way, it can work powerfully in both directions. This relationship can be seen as an advancement of mentoring, when mentoring develops into a two-way process of influence and then further to one of collaborative working relationships and co-learning (Graen and Scandura, 1987; Kram and Hall, 1995). The

Dynamic Duos collaboration can manifest in the workplace through the relationship between Social Intrapreneur and Godparent.

5.3.3 Overcoming powerlessness

A comment many middle managers make is that they feel disempowered into action, that they do not have enough power to make a difference. They may agree that sustainability is important and that climate change is a significant problem, but they do not see how they personally can make a difference – they can 'switch off' to the problems because they don't see effective solutions or how they can make a difference. This feeling of powerlessness can discourage and create apathy, and can exist for a variety of reasons, such as macro-level issues (Gallup Engagement Index, 2010) of a more general 'engagement gap' in business, or personal issues such as perceived unfairness (Sharma *et al.*, 2009) or a general lack of justice and trust in their managers (Chiaburu and Lim, 2008). Further, often both clear organisational values as well as individual concern for the issues usually need to be present – especially with natural environmental issues – for an employee to be driven to address an issue. This combination of the two is not always present (Bansal, 2003). This feeling of powerlessness is very different to the other change-makers profiled in the book, who are active in understanding their place in the world and take control or power to make a difference. Although Godparents Justin and Cassiano are active change-makers, this does not have to be a motivational driver for other potential Godparents – in fact, becoming a sustainability Godparent can be a way of middle and senior managers gaining some power.

Power is discussed throughout this book, and a middle manager can have power in a few forms that they may not recognise. As a Sustainability Godparent they can utilise this power. See 'Advice to Godparents' below for more information on this, but the following ancient African proverb is relevant:

> If you think you are too small to make a difference, try sleeping in a closed room with a mosquito.

5.4 Advice for Godparents

The role of a Sustainability Godparent can be quite low in impact, although Justin and Cassiano did get passionate about their protégés and the work they were doing. What is important is to set clear expectations of what the Godparent can contribute, and in turn what the protégé can contribute. This does not necessarily need a formal system for Godparenting, as for some employees this can be restricting, but it could mean having discussions about the relationship and expectations – especially if so far the relationship has emerged organically. Therefore, it does help either to decide proactively to be a Godparent and contact the HR or Sustainability team, or (if already mentoring a protégé or being sent more junior employees because you hold specialist knowledge from which a sustainability change agent could benefit) having a specific discussion with your protégé about what you are willing to contribute, what the protégé's objectives are, what help is needed and how the relationship could operate.

5.4.1 Low-effort Godparenting

Any organisation will have legitimate systems as well as tactics or informal systems for how things get done. Whether by (for example) power-brokering, story-telling,[5] ceremonies involved when seeking approval or building alliances, there will be formal and informal ways of achieving tasks (Buchanan and Huczynski, 1997).[6] Godparents, who will tend to be more experienced and aware of how these shadow systems work, can utilise these systems for their protégé (Houchin and MacLean, 2005).

The most fundamental role a Godparent can take is to be a critical friend – a 'sounding board' for the protégé's ideas and how the individual articulates ideas. Often employees build their perception of a situation based on the 'lens' they have of the business and environment. This means if they do not have access to certain information they run the risk of their credibility being harmed if they present a case that is flawed because it misses that key piece of information (Whitehouse, 2006). A Godparent can be someone to share relevant knowledge with the less experienced employee (Swap *et al.*, 2001) – either about sustainability or about how to pitch ideas, build a business case and write a proposal. A protégé can present ideas to a Godparent for feedback precisely to highlight missed knowledge, technical detail and business sense. Likewise, sometimes the articulation of the idea is where a Godparent can help; a Godparent is well positioned to understand the language used in the firm and know what issues are on the corporate agenda or how the idea can be connected with an issue on the corporate agenda. This is especially relevant in terms of talking in the language of the audience, in the unique context and bounded views of the organisation's members (Balogun *et al.*, 2005). Cassiano once attached a sticker to Lucas's (his protégé at Danone) computer screen saying 'Stop being fluffy' – challenging Lucas to express his ideas more in business language. Lucas still keeps the sticker at home to remind him of this important learning.[7]

An easy role that the Godparent can take is as story-teller. As a legitimate organisational actor, the Godparent has an established network and relevance to other employees. By sharing with other key employees the ideas and opportunities of the protégé the Godparent is legitimising the protégé's efforts and giving a 'seal of approval'. This can greatly enable a sustainability change-maker who may be new, young or of lower rank and taking action to change the status quo on a subject that may not yet be defined or legitimate in the organisation. By talking about sustainability as a legitimate and relevant concept (called 'managing meaning'), the Godparent can further the organisational understanding and acceptance of sustainability – precisely because the Godparent is a legitimate and accepted figure in the organisation (Valentino and Francis, 2004).

> I had many talks with e.g. sales people that their children are aware of [issues such as] recycling and they can tell them now that their employer is doing something.
>
> (Cassiano)

5.4.2 Proactive Godparenting

Sustainability Godparents can take on a more proactive position if they also have a passion for corporate sustainability, or a specific issue within that. For example, at Danone Cassiano proactively looked for junior members of staff who were interested in sustainability and also had business skills. Building a network internally with the Sustainability department can create a powerful network of protégés that together could make real change within the organisation. This not only aids the protégé and potential protégés but also creates a unique identity within the organisation for the Godparent.

Some Godparents proactively create new reporting structures for their protégés so that they have enough discretion within their job to be able to work on proposals, research and develop ideas and even run small experimental projects. This can be easier if the Godparent is a line manager or senior member of staff who can influence those who line-manage the protégé. Some Godparents change the organisational rules so that the idea or project is given a chance to prove itself – as seen with Justin (Arup). This is something common in sustainable business because the very nature of sustainable projects is that they can still be new in approach, mindset, return and execution. Some organisations set up innovation funds to do precisely this and recruit a committee of employees and external experts to adjudicate and reward the winners (who are then given a set budget to develop a detailed business plan). Sustainable projects can have longer pay-back times or different success metrics and often Godparents can use their influence to adjust the metrics to be more relevant for long-term holistic thinking. Sometimes this involves ring fencing a project as an experiment – something a Godparent with positional power can do – or negotiating with Finance, project supervisors or even the protégé's line manager so that the protégé has more flexibility to experiment and be innovative.

> What I helped her do was to establish international development, ring fencing it and setting it up as a non-profit business within the firm with a different business model and overhead structure.
>
> (Justin, Arup)

A Godparent can also share power or authority with the protégé. This is a potentially powerful tactic to use, but requires a good degree of trust to exist between protégé and Godparent. Related to the advice given to Social Intrapreneurs on power, Godparents can:

1. *Lend power to their protégé*: there is power inherent in the organisation's system, such as power to sign off budgets or proposals. This power can be lent to the protégé they trust, for a period of time (Balogun *et al.*, 2005). This was seen with Justin (Arup), who helped manoeuvre Jo so that she could develop into a Director with ArupID being an independent cost centre.

2. *Share their earned authority*: the protégé may not have yet earned positional power or authority but middle managers who are known, know how the organisation works and have proven themselves to be good at their job will have earned authority, even if this is not overtly 'ranked' power. They have earned the moral authority (Lawrence *et al.*, 2006), or credibility, to take action. As Sustainability Godparents they can utilise that authority, or lend it to their protégé by simply making it known that they support the work the protégé is doing, and make introductions to the decision-makers for the protégé (Zald, 2005). Justin (Arup) took this further and used his access to the board to argue Jo's case for ArupID.

3. *Utilise their own positional power*: formal power is usually given with positions, such as senior ranks or line management. Middle or senior managers will typically have some sort of power though the ranking system in the organisation, whether resources such as budget or because of their reporting line (Balogun *et al.*, 2005) and so having access to senior people. This was seen with Cassiano, who at the time connected Lucas with the Vice President of Innovation and R&D in Danone. Godparents can utilise the idea of 'Dynamic Duos' and make strategic connections for their protégés.

4. Themselves take *entrepreneurial* power to help their protégé. This is when managers take power without permission in order to carry out their job.[8] This can be by quietly adding tasks or actions to their day role, enlisting a powerful stakeholder or arguing the case on behalf of their protégé so effectively that they are given discretion to scope out the idea as a new enterprise. If not carefully done this can be disruptive (in a negative or positive way). However, Cassiano (formerly Danone) is an example of this being done in a positive way, by actively looking for trainees in the corporate training programme who had a passion for business and sustainability and were entrepreneurial; and by incorporating sustainability into the talks he gave to potential graduates – part of his 'Machiavellian plan'.

5.5 Advice for organisations

Undertaking the commitment to become a sustainable organisation, whilst obviously positive, is a significant commitment. The CEO and other organisational leaders need to commit to the process, engage employees across the organisation and make a significant commitment to audit and improve, where necessary, the organisation's purpose, strategy, tactics and operations. However, not all employees will be engaged in the process. The relationship individuals want with their place of work varies, and many may look to other places in their life for their sources of meaning. Some employees may want a transactional exchange with an organisation (a reciprocal relationship where time/effort is exchanged for a specific benefit), others a relational exchange (work contributes to and strengthens their own identity, who they are) and others a developmental relationship (work gives opportunity for purpose to individuals, who they wish to be: Mirvis, 2012). A transactional relationship is common; many do not look for their place of work to be challenging or complex or to seek out platforms at work where they can make significant change. Therefore, not all employees will want to be active change-makers. How can those tasked with creating sustainable organisations engage employees in that context?

Two key ways are explored in this book – notably Chapter 1 (Unsung Heroes) and the work leading UK retailer Marks & Spencer did to engage employees. However, the role of a Godparent can be another way that less interested employees can be engaged in, for motivations other than a passion for sustainability such as mentoring or developing skills of junior team members. For them, being a Godparent can be a positive way to be part of the organisation's change journey. However, change-makers such as the leaders of the organisation and the Sustainability Specialist need to create an 'environment' and tools where these middle managers can become Sustainability Godparents.

5.5.1 Clarifying and communicating embedded enablers

Managers tend to focus on a narrow set of responsibilities at work that are closely related to the operations of the firm – what is seen as relevant to the firm (Bansal, 2003). Many also will perceive the issues that they can address (have 'permission to address') by signals sent by organisational actors (Hayes, 2007). For example, if a CEO does not talk about sustainability – or does so in narrow terms not related to daily operations – then employees can interpret this as a signal that sustainability is not relevant. There are embedded enablers that leaders, the HR team and Sustainability Specialists can utilise and communicate to help all employees be aware and know they have permission to engage. Not all employees will then engage, but by providing options – regardless of motivations – more Godparents could emerge. Therefore, the leaders of the organisations need to:

1. Clearly espouse the values of the organisation and how they are relevant to operations, and then talk about how sustainability supports these values. For example, a value of 'respect' or 'integrity' can easily be connected to a human rights code of conduct or signing up to Fairtrade standards. Providing specific examples – 'symbolic acts' – can encourage potential Godparents to take on new actions that are in line with those values, such as enabling and supporting colleagues.

2. The leaders of the organisation also need to talk about the agenda for change, and encourage this language to cascade through the organisations through the tactic and formal communication systems. Called 'tone from the top', the extent to which sustainability is championed by management is important (Collier and Esteban, 2007). Several leading CEOs have held successful road shows, where they visit every office, shop and warehouse over a period of a year and present to employees what the change agenda is. External communications to stakeholders, speeches, presentations, public relations materials and annual reports also need to use the language of change to reinforce that the sustainability agenda is legitimate. If this can be established, then strong signals will be sent to employees that they have permission to support sustainability change and the employees who are taking specific actions to embed sustainability. Academic and change management guru John Kotter (1995) urges:

   • Establish a sense of urgency and find ways to communicate this.
   • Create a powerful guiding coalition of senior internal employees, with power and legitimacy.
   • Provide a vision (change agenda) that employees can visualise and follow.
   • Communicate, communicate, communicate.

3. However, it is important for sustainability to be defined at a concept level, so that meaning is given relevance to the company and departments. Employees need to know how sustainability is relevant and therefore how initiatives will impact the organisation (Whitehouse, 2006). This helps employees to make sense of sustainability in their context, but, importantly, also helps them to frame what they can engage with and what will motivate them (called sense-making). Making it clear that all employees have a role, but that different roles are available and are not prescriptive – and providing examples, such as a call for mentors – can encourage middle managers to engage.

5.5.2 Specific tools

Specific tools can be developed to encourage and help middle and senior manager (passionate or not about sustainability – although the case studies do show those with an interest are highly effective) to become Sustainability

Godparents. The organisation's Learning and Development teams are especially relevant, as they will be responsible for programmes that can be 'piggy-backed',[9] such as the employee trainee programme, the 'fast-track' management programme or an existing mentoring programme. These existing activities can be platforms for potential Godparent–protégé relationships. The position of mentor can be seen as a reward and a status symbol if the programme is set up well and spoken about by leaders of the organisation – those who become Godparents can be rewarded with profiles in internal newsletters, specific mention by the CEO and other such recognition-based rewards. Related learning aids can be provided such as information packs on a dedicated section of the intranet with frequently asked questions, common tips and advice sheets.

The Sustainability Specialists can also set up similar specific sustainability-branded programmes for change agents and senior or experienced members of the organisation; these can take on a Dynamic Duo set-up. Volunteers can be found or senior directors can nominate potential Godparents and identify possible protégés, for example from the Champions network. Several organisations have mentoring programmes specifically for their Sustainability Champions which work well in helping Champions navigate the political processes of the organisation (Exter, 2009).

It is important to provide any such programme with support and training for the Godparent and protégé. There are many guidebooks, toolkits and courses advising on how to mentor, which could be useful sources of training.

5.6 Concluding thoughts

It is only in recent research that the employee type 'Sustainability Godparent' has been identified. Unlike the other employee types identified in the book, Godparents may not be driven to help because of a personal interest in sustainable business. They may not want to be change-makers. However, what is clear so far is that they are motivated to share their expertise and derive satisfaction from enabling other employees to be successful in their efforts to create change. The Godparent does not need specialist knowledge of sustainability – and can even take low-effort actions which can still have positive results. Others can take proactive action which can greatly help other change-makers to create significant impact. Thus, this is a role that middle or senior managers can take on if they are concerned about the environment and society but feel that they are unsuited to be proactive change-makers or if they want some power to influence their surroundings that they feel is currently lacking. The middle-management 'black hole' need not be the 'treacle' where great initiatives and ideas get lost, if we all – in our own way – help.

5.6.1 Summary advice

- A Godparent can help to make significant change in small simple ways: by utilising the legitimacy, power and influence they have in their organisation.
- More involved Godparents can be the critical success factor for enabling other change-makers in their success. They can be proactive Godparents.
- Sustainability Godparents do not necessarily have to have a personal passion for sustainability. They could be passionate about developing future generations, enabling others or a specific team member, or enjoy sharing their wisdom.
- Organisations on the sustainability journey should encourage key middle and senior managers (especially those with power and authority) to become Godparents – it is a way of engaging the middle layer of the organisation who may not be positioned or motivated to understand why the organisation is working to be sustainable.
- For individuals, the role can provide fresh contacts, insights, motivation and interest into their day job.
- Formal mentoring programmes can be established, but for Godparents specifically both the HR and Sustainability teams should work together to develop, encourage and also provide the right skills and tools for Godparents.
- Godparents and protégés should share with each other their hopes for the relationship and what each is willing to put into the relationship.
- Godparent/mentor relationships tend to work better with a good degree of mutual trust, respect and clarity.
- For the protégé, a Godparent can teach valuable and unique skills for creating change. The Godparent can enable the protégé to access people and resource that otherwise might not be available. At the least, the Godparent can be someone to test ideas on and advise on how to present the case for a related project or idea.

Final thoughts

Throughout this book case study after case study profiles what a collection of extraordinary employees are doing to change the world. They share why they express their values and address their concerns through their place of work. The Unsung Heroes, Specialists, Champions, Social Intrapreneurs and Godparents are good examples to follow. I hope the stories inspire you, because now it is your turn; our future is in your hands.

Climate change fatigue, melancholia, confusion or denial is no longer acceptable. Predictions for the future are varied, but in relation to climate change all the probable scenarios come with a heavy price to be paid. In 2009 Nicholas Stern published a book entitled *A Blueprint for a Safer Planet* in which he showed what would occur at each average one-degree temperature rise during this century, and the consequent environmental, social and economic impacts (Stern, 2008, 2009):[1]

- Average two-degree rise in global temperatures: one-third of the world's species becomes extinct. Regular summer heat waves in south England will see 40-degree temperatures. In the summer months the Amazon forest will be desert and grasslands. There will be significant coastal flooding across the world with expected migration and economic impacts, and oceans will be too acidic for the remaining coral reefs to survive, impacting on the food chain in (and from) the oceans. *This is the rise in temperature limit from human activity that politicians globally are still struggling to agree to, and take the correct action for.*
- Average three-degree rise in global temperatures: widespread deserts in South Africa, Australia and Western USA. About 30–50% less water available in Africa and the Mediterranean. Mass migration, economic impacts and refugees. This is the temperature rise at which scientists fear global warming will no longer be controllable by humanity.
- Average four-degree rise in global temperatures: many islands submerged. Italy, Spain, Greece and Turkey are deserts. Temperatures in Europe regularly up to 50 degrees.

- Average five-degree rise in global temperatures: this is the nightmare scenario with widespread species extinction, loss of land mass and massive number of climate refugees.

The US Intergovernmental Panel on Climate Change Special Report on Emissions Scenario predicts:

> a best estimate of global temperature increase of 1.8–4.0°C with a possible range of 1.1–6.4°C by 2100.[2]

The impacts are not just environmental: the social and economic implications are significant and compound existing issues[3] such as the gap between rich and poor, growing social and intergenerational injustice, and already existing limitations on raw materials for food, clothing, consumables and land for farming and homes. The 2012 DARA report estimated that five million lives are already being lost each year as a result of climate change, and that the poorest nations will be the ones most impacted. Climate change is already setting back global development by 1% of world gross domestic product (GDP) – in 2010 poorer countries specifically were losing up to 7% of their GDP because of inaction to climate change. Even the USA will lose more than 2% of its GDP by 2030 because of climate change (DARA, 2012).

One could be forgiven for also having a negative view of the role of business in society when considering the scandals of the last decade. Highlights include the Enron scandal in 2001; the global financial crash in 2007–8 (widely agreed that the irresponsible corporate practices of banks and the financial community was a significant cause); concerns (especially in the USA and Europe) over tax practices and avoidance of multinational organisations; human rights and labour scandals in Asia (specifically, more recently public trust in business in Japan[4]) and the impact of corporate acquisition of natural resources in developing economies such as Africa (resulting in shortages, price rises and food riots in Africa). Public trust in business globally has fallen significantly in the last decade, as seen via the Edelman trust barometer:

- In 2012, trust in business fell globally from 2011, to an average of 53% of respondents saying they trust business to do the right thing; 49% of respondents said governments do not regulate business enough (Edelman, 2012).

Recent discussion in the political, business, activist and academic spheres is focusing on the need for system-level change, a 'course correction' for capitalism and a re-examining of the typical business models of corporations. The Harvard Business School, via their publication *Harvard Business Review* and online community, is a good barometer of the critical conversations taking place in the business world. They have a series of very active ongoing conversations about 'rethinking capitalism', 'fixing capitalism', and more specifically, the role of business leaders in fixing the capitalist and market systems ('the CEO's [Chief Executive Officer's] role in fixing the system'):

> for some baffling reason, we persistently stop short of questioning *the underlying structure of the firm itself*. That structure is at the heart of the problem – it's the DNA of capitalism. Until we address it, we're just treating symptoms, and our reform efforts will not reach the scale and speed required to avert the looming storm.
>
> (Sabeti, 2011)

> business leaders must take a more active role in protecting and improving the system . . . They must help devise strategies that provide employment for the billions now outside the system, which, in turn, means changing how they think about the relationship between productivity and profit. They must invent business models that make better use of scarce resources and even take advantage of looming resource shortages. And they must create institutional arrangements for coordinating and governing neglected and dysfunctional aspects of market capitalism.
>
> (Bower *et al.*, 2011)

What the business and political conversations will actually result in is very uncertain. Although more than four-fifths of respondents ($n = 405$) from the Global 500 companies[5] identify physical risks to their business from rising temperatures, the average annual reduction on carbon pollution from this group is still only 1% (CPD Global 500 Climate Change report, 2012). Will real and positive change occur? Or will the rhetoric–reality gap continue in this decade as well? Whether it is rhetoric or action that occurs, we must remember that business is made up of people who are members of the sceptical public – members of civil society. In other words: you and me. Over three billion people around the world work (International Labour Office, 2012). We cannot blame faceless corporations; businesses are not run by automated machines or mystical beings, but by people who live next door to you, who shop in the same supermarket as you and whose children go to the same school as your children. We cannot divorce bad business behaviour from ourselves because we are part of their global workforce. And just as we are part of the problem, we are also part of the solution. By taking back control of how our society works, of the role that we – through business – have in society, then we can be part of a world that works for all.

And many of us are doing this. There have in the last decade been significant breakthroughs in corporate reporting and accounting for (and therefore minimising of) negative environmental, social and governance impacts and maximising positive ones – the true cost of the impact companies have on society and environment;[6] in the number of listed companies addressing sustainability more strategically (in 2012 89% of FTSE100 companies had a board member specifically responsible for sustainability issues[7]); and in the innovative solutions businesses are creating to address environmental and social constraints.[8] Many academics and scientists propose that global challenges are becoming a prime driver of innovation for business, as seen with the emergence of mobile banking and micro lending from employees seeking to match business opportunity with social benefit (Mirvis and Googins, 2012). These breakthroughs have occurred because of the employees working inside these businesses; people from every walk of life are more readily standing up and committing to sustainable action. A collection of examples are described in this book – real people who have taken control of the impact they have on the world through where they work. These are the positive stories we need to share.

What is occurring in civil society – and is arguably more interesting and impactful than political discussions – is the *global sustainability social movement within civil society*. An overarching sustainability movement that is manifesting in smaller social movements such as the Uncut movement; boycotts against multinationals partaking in socially unacceptable behaviour (from tax avoidance to human rights violations and wildlife endangerment); and a growth in alternative business models such as social enterprises, B-corporations, co-ops, mutuals and community or employee-owned businesses[9] which could in our future change the very definition of what a typical corporation is. Throughout this book this concept of 'Sustainability social movement' is described and it is argued that the employees profiled here are manifestations of this social movement. This is what we need to be talking about – mainstreaming sustainability into everyday mindset and behaviours, from the grassroots up, in work but also at home. Because this is where the real power, the real-time ability to make a difference, sits. This is where you can really change the world without losing your day job.

You can easily take action now – make a commitment to the Saatchi & Saatchi Do One Thing campaign (www.strategyforsustainability.com/do-one-thing/). Contact the leaders of your organisation and ask them what the organisation does to be sustainable. Use your power as a consumer to tell businesses what is important to you and what you feel their responsibilities are. But above all, assess your actions and see how you can change your behaviour to be more sustainable – often in very small ways – and how you can actively reinforce your values and concerns in your day job. Take back control.

10 Simple Things to Take Back Control

1. Stay informed – read, watch, and listen. Knowledge *is* power!

2. Make a commitment to the Do One Thing Campaign – and do it!

3. Ask the leaders of your organisation what your organisation does to be sustainable; is this something you are proud of or want improved?

4. Identify what interests you, whether for example conservation or human rights, and find and build a network of other employees at work also interested.

5. Audit your own life, at home and at work, and if you find anything you are not proud of – change what you can!

6. Ask for help on commitments that you make – you are not alone. There is lots of free advice available.

7. Be a proactive consumer – do your research and support through your purchases, and tell businesses why you will no longer support them.

8. When surveyed, or have an opportunity to vote/comment on responsible and sustainable practices whether at work, home or in public policy – do!

9. If you have a great idea, be brave – articulate it, build a business case, and get support for testing it out.

10. Finally . . . take time to enjoy and appreciate what is great, and what we want to keep, in society and the natural environment!

Notes

You too can make a difference

1. For projections specific to the environment, see DARA (2012), MIT Global Climate Solutions Model (2012) and Rockström *et al.* (2009).
2. For a future visioning in film, see *The Age of Stupid*.
3. For more on climate change fatigue and blame-shifting, read Weintrobe (2013).
4. Formal and informal process and procedures that dictate or guide how things get done in the organisation.
5. For example, prior to the 2012 Rio+20 Conference on Sustainable Development, a group of over 1,000 businesses leaders from very large global multinationals together made significant voluntary corporate commitments to be more sustainable.
6. With a global population in 2012 over seven billion (including those not of working age, unemployed and unable to work), in fact all can get involved, whether employed or not.

Introduction

1. Term used in the Brundtland Report, meaning our attempts to improve our situation (quality of life, status, financial stability, etc.).
2. See Business in The Community for further info on this categorisation of impacts: http://www.bitc.org.uk/issues.
3. Environmentalism concerns have existed throughout history but in more recent times the United Nations (UN) first met to discuss the environment in 1972 (UN Conference on Human Environment), and the Brundtland Report (United Nations, 1987) defined and made 'sustainability' a legitimate and critical political matter to be managed at a global level.
4. A few landmark early books in new social movement seen as a marker of modern environmentalism are: *A Sand County Almanac* by ecologist Aldo Leopard (Leopard, 1949); *The Silent Spring* by Rachel Carson (Carson, 1962) and *Gaia: A New Look at Life on Earth* by scientist James Lovelock (Lovelock, 1979).
5. With thanks to colleague Melody McLaren for contributions to the developmental stage model.
6. Otherwise called 'collectives' in social identity theory and theory of collectivistic tendencies.
7. For more reading on organisational culture, see writings by academics Deal and Kennedy (1982), Kotter (1995), Ravasi and Schultz (2006) and Schein (2010).
8. Barclays Bank is an example of recognising a bad culture and wanting to fix it. See *Guardian* Newspapers (UK) 17 January 'Barclays boss tells staff: sign up to new values or leave' (article now out of copyright) and 5 February 2013 'Barclays

boss dumps on Bob Diamond'. Online at: http://www.guardian.co.uk/business/2013/feb/05/barclays-antony-jenkins-bob-diamond (accessed March 2013).

1 Unsung Heroes

1. An initiative launched by M&S in 2012 in partnership with Oxfam to encourage customers to bring in unused clothing items, whether bought from M&S or not, for resale, reuse or recycling via Oxfam.
2. When the M&S culture is described in this chapter, this refers to dominant culture.
3. Kweku Adoboli was found guilty of fraud on 20 November: http://www.bbc.co.uk/news/uk-20338042 (accessed 20 November 2012).
4. The legitimate systems are those that are formal and written down. The shadow, or informal, systems are behaviours or motivations that occur informally (Houchin and MacLean, 2005).
5. For more information on how regional culture affects organisational culture and employees, see Hofstede's (1984) dimensions of culture.
6. Schein (2010) identified three levels: the tip as artefacts that can be seen; espoused values; and basic underlying assumptions that are taken for granted but not seen (and under the water line).
7. See, for example, the Culture Web (Johnson and Scholes, 2005).
8. Failure of cultural integration or underestimating the difficulty of cultural integration and associated risks is cited as a reason for many mergers and acquisitions failures (Weber, 1996).
9. This is from a resource-based view of the firm: see for further reading Barney (1991).
10. 'Engagement' refers to when employees have a voice, are motivated to identify with the organisation and develop a sense of pride from the association. Engagement is a two-way process that is maintained. Communications is a tool for engagement, but communications on its own is not engagement.
11. Drawing on observations from own experience advising large consultancies that are target-driven.
12. 'Nudge' refers to efforts to move people towards making better decisions, from Thaler (2008).
13. Internal material provided by M&S.
14. Internal M&S document: Engagement delivers . . . do you? April 2012.
15. For more information on specific areas on which the Plan A team are working to embed sustainability, see http://plana.marksandspencer.com/media/pdf/ms_hdwb_2012.pdf, p. 16.

2 The corporate Sustainability Specialist

1. Judge Keady served as judge from 1968 until his death in 1989. He 'is widely regarded as having single-handedly forced the state to improve its deteriorating prisons, especially the Mississippi State Penitentiary in Parchman and also handed down significant rulings favoring desegregation of public schools' (*Chicago Tribune News*, 18 June 1989).
2. 'Bottom of the pyramid' refers to the poorest, but largest, socioeconomic group of about three billion people who live on less than US$2.50 a day (Global Issues, 2013).
3. A process used by many businesses to identify and prioritise the management of material impacts (Cormack, 2012).
4. Still a closed enclave at that time – Berlin was cut off from Western Europe by the Berlin Wall, as a separate region, and as such its citizens were not privy to many of the rights of other citizens of Germany.

5. Sudden deregulation and withdrawal of financial support for the airline industry by the Conservative government in the UK during the 1980s.

6. A management process that looks to eliminate waste and better provide goods and services (George, 2002).

7. A 1992 Argentinean film directed by Adolfo Aristarain.

8. For a profile of the NBI, see Grayson and Nelson (2013).

9. 'Net positive impact' refers initially to environmental impact, but has been extended to include all impacts. For further reading, see: www.greenbiz.com/blog/2012/02/09/next-smart-sustainability-idea-net-positive-impact-business.

10. See, for example, writings by Gilman (1990), Senge (2008), Touraine (1985), Waddock (2008) and, of course, Elkington (1997, 2008b) and reports and research on macro trends from academies, think tanks and government departments in Europe, North America, Latin America and Asia (see also articles in *Harvard Business Review*).

11. Learned needs: what is learned from coping with one's environment in childhood which helps to create one's value system. For further reading on learned needs in relation to taking action for sustainability in later life, see Bansal (2003).

12. Even for those with a clear sense of self, including values and characteristics, the degree to which individuals will allow this sense to be compromised in a job role varies. Some, for example, have a higher tolerance for some characteristics to be compromised but may be rigid that the organisation and job cannot compromise a specific set of values. This is called 'flexible' or 'fixed'.

13. The human animal has collectivistic tendencies, the degrees of which differ because of psychological characteristics of the individual, and social efficacy and situational influences such as region/culture: for example, Americans tend towards individualism in comparison to Japanese people, who tend towards collectivism (Kobayashi *et al.*, 2010). This shapes our desires for group working or individual autonomy, and the degree to which we buy-into the organisation's goals and values. It affects our motivation to collaborate (Song, 2009).

14. 'Horizon scanning': the systematic examination of potential threats, opportunities and likely developments including, but not restricted to, those at the margins of current thinking and planning. Horizon scanning may explore novel and unexpected issues as well as persistent problems or trends (OSI, 2008).

15. C-suite refers to the executive level of an organisation where employees with the word 'Chief' typically are ranked, such as Chief Executive Officer and Chief Finance Officer.

16. See Kingfisher CEO video and introduction for their 2012 report: www.kingfisher.com/netpositive/index.asp?pageid=14.

17. Unpublished research (2012) from the Doughty Centre on the governance of sustainability. See also BITC and Doughty Centre for Corporate Responsibility (2013).

18. Mainly from studies in the UK and continental Europe and Asia (Acre, Acona, 2012; Boston College Centre for Corporate Citizenship, 2012).

19. Widely used in budgeting. IRR = internal rate of return for an investment. NPV = net present value, a central tool in discounted cash flow analysis and a standard method for using the time value of money to appraise viability of investment in long-term projects.

20. For more information on the business case for being a responsible business, see Doughty Centre for Corporate Responsibility and BITC (2011), PWC (2012) and Ferguson (2010). Environmental profit and losses are available: see integrated reporting or true cost accounting. Integrated reporting is a process that results in communication, most visibly a periodic 'integrated report', about value creation over time. It integrates all aspects of value creation and impact (financial and non-financial) of a business, across social, environmental and economic areas,

so that there can be better decision-making. True cost accounting is when the full costs of a product or service are reflected in the price, including social and economic costs. True cost accounting is a method for accounting for economic costs that would normally be treated as an externality (an impact and cost seen as external to the price of the item) and otherwise be covered by nature or society.

21. 'Insurgency' relates to prosocial bureaucratic insurgency, where managers and professionals with strong identities commandeer organisational resources to create change. When sanctioned, this can serve social and organisational interests, in comparison to unsanctioned insurgency, which can be destructive (Zald, 2005).

22. Based on the observation of when entrepreneurial discretion meets bureaucratic insurgency, i.e. when managers, in an entrepreneurial spirit and with a degree of job discretion, take power without approval to accomplish something they feel is for the good of the company.

23. Managerial discretion has been seen to be an important component of corporate responsibility when allocating resources (Collier and Esteban, 2007). Conversely, the degree of autonomy and exercise of choice are drivers of behaviour.

3 The Social Intrapreneur

1. The team – Professor David Grayson, Associate Professor Heiko Spitzeck, Dr Elisa Alt and Melody McLaren – have also produced a 2013 paper (see references).

2. USAID works in over 100 countries to: promote broadly shared economic prosperity; strengthen democracy and good governance; protect human rights; improve global health, advance food security and agriculture; improve environmental sustainability; further education; help societies prevent and recover from conflicts; and provide humanitarian assistance in the wake of natural and man-made disasters (www.usaid.gov).

3. A global think tank of regional and global politicians, and prominent members from civil society, the scientific community and business. It released the report *The Limits to Growth* in 1972 (Meadows *et al.*, 1972), the report (now a book) discussed the global unchecked economic and population growth occurring within finite resource supplies.

4. For more information, see www.arup.com/Home/Publications/The_Key_Speech. aspx.

5. Initiatives launched by the then Labour government: Sure Start focused on the improvement of childcare, early education, health and family support, with an emphasis on outreach and community development. The Academies programme was an initiative with a focus on improving failing government-funded schools, partly sponsored by private sponsors and run independently of local authorities.

6. One of the largest global natural disasters recorded, it occurred on 26 December 2004. A massive tsunami in the Indian Ocean, initiated by the third-largest earthquake ever recorded, killed over 230,000 people in over 14 countries. Especially hit were Indonesia, Sri Lanka, India and Thailand.

7. Accenture Development Partnerships (ADP), a not-for-profit business arm of Accenture Consulting with a focus on international development, initiated by Gib Bulloch, another Social Intrapreneur.

8. Inclusive business: creating sustainable livelihoods and providing affordable goods and services that meet a social or environmental need whilst generating business opportunity.

9. 'Shared value' is a term used by Nestlé to describe its sustainability mindset, and defined by Porter and Kramer (2011) as: 'The concept of shared value can be defined as policies and operating practices that enhance the competitiveness of

a company while simultaneously advancing the economic and social conditions in the communities in which it operates. Shared value creation focuses on identifying and expanding the connections between societal and economic progress.'

10. For more case studies, see Grayson *et al.* (2013).
11. To read more on the motivations behind making a difference specifically for sustainability, see Visser (2008).
12. Now with the consulting firm Imaginals (www.imaginals.net) and one of the authors of the 2008 Social Intrapreneurs field guide (Elkington, 2008a).
13. Unsanctioned bureaucratic insurgency, based on entrepreneurial discretion and bureaucratic insurgency.
14. Managerial discretion has been seen to be an important component of corporate responsibility when allocating resources (Collier and Esteban, 2007). Conversely, the degree of autonomy and exercise of choice is a driver of behaviour.
15. Where feedback on an employee's performance – social, collective as well as task-oriented – is collated from all key stakeholders the employees work with, inside and often outside the organisation as well.

4 The Sustainability Champion

1. Inspired by a musical stairs in Stockholm: www.youtube.com/watch?v=ipMib6ejGuo.
2. *Captain Planet and the Planeteers* is an American animated environmentalist television programme which was broadcast on TBS from 1990 to 1996, with a sequel, *The New Adventures of Captain Planet*, that ran initially for three seasons. Both series continue today in syndication.
3. 'Shared value' is a term used by Nestlé to describe its sustainability mindset, and defined by Porter and Kramer (2011).
4. However it was observed in the research that most Champions are respected in their main role, both before they take on Champion tasks and because of the tasks they take on. And some Champions do experience personal success such as promotion, opportunity or recognition. Marks & Spencer, which established a Plan A Champions network for all its stores in 2009, has found that the network is proving to be an additional source of candidates for its management fast-track programme.
5. For further information on this desire to make a difference, see writings on 'ego expression' (the desire to express your unique self that makes you distinct from the world) (Amos and Weathington, 2008). To assess your individual orientation towards work, see Schein (2006).
6. For further information on how corporate sustainability can develop employee commitment, read about 'affective commitment' (Collier and Esteban, 2007).
7. For example, from expectations for how we work, the culture and values of the organisation, the opportunities we have and the level of challenge from the job.
8. See Bendell (2009) and writings of sustainability specialist John Elkington.
9. The view they form that is shaped by their rank and physical position and the information they have access to.
10. To hear something through the grapevine is verbally to learn of something informally and unofficially, such as by gossip and rumour.
11. For more information on this, see Exter (2011).

5 The Sustainability Godparent

1. Interview conducted in 2011.
2. A Social Intrapreneur, profiled in Chapter 3.

3. Lucas is Sustainability Manager at Danone (2012) and a social Intrapreneur identified in the research. See Grayson *et al.* (2013) and Introduction for more on this.
4. A consortium of Volans, Cranfield University and Accenture: www.volans.com/lab/projects/ageing/.
5. For more information on story-telling, see McLaren M (2010). Supporting corporate responsibility performance through effective knowledge management. The Doughty Centre for Corporate Responsibility.
6. Often called the 'subculture' (Buchanan and Huczynski, 1997) or shadow systems (Houchin and MacLean, 2005).
7. From interview with Lucas Urbano, Sustainability Manager of Danone, in 2011.
8. 'Bureaucratic insurgents': a relatively small group of middle managers and professionals working partially to change products, processes or policies from within. Unsanctioned bureaucratic insurgency is when this action has not been specifically sanctioned by the leaders, and is based on the combination of entrepreneurial discretion and bureaucratic insurgency (Zald, 2005).
9. Utilising existing processes, expectations and projects for sustainability-related activities. Having related systems in place that are seen as legitimate by the organisation can help to legitimise the activity as well as provide familiarity for employees so that the activity is unthreatening.

Final thoughts

1. For the UK Treasury Office, see http://www.hm-treasury.gov.uk/d/Executive_Summary.pdf.
2. National Oceanic and Atmospheric Administration and National Climatic Data Center summary of 2007 Fourth Assessment Report (AR4) by the US Intergovernmental Panel on Climate Change (IPCC), as well as NCDC's own data resources. See www.ncdc.noaa.gov/cmb-faq/globalwarming.html#q13.
3. For US-specific scenarios, see www.epa.gov/climatechange/science/future.html.
4. Notably in Japan after the Olympus scandal exposed by the now deposed CEO, Michael Woodford. See also Edelman (2012).
5. Report written on behalf of investors who together have assets of over US$78 trillion.
6. See True Cost accounting and the debates around corporations paying for the impacts they create (www.guardian.co.uk/environment/2010/feb/18/worlds-top-firms-environmental-damage) and integrated reporting (www.theiirc.org/).
7. Unpublished research from the Doughty Centre on the governance of sustainability, 2012.
8. Such as agricultural innovations (i.e. biotech seeding), gene therapy, carbon calculating, synthetic DNA, wind power and alternative energy storage and three-dimensional printing. See *Stanford Social Innovation Review* for case studies and research on social innovation.
9. For example, over one billion people worldwide are members of co-operatives. 2012 was the International Year of the Co-operative: http://social.un.org/coopsyear/.

References

Acre, Acona (2012). *Ethical Performance and Flag The CR and Sustainability Salary Survey.* Online at: http://crsalarysurvey.com/_media/documents/survey12.pdf (accessed March 2013).

Amos E, Weathington B (2008). An analysis of the relation between employee-organisation value congruence and employee attitudes. *Journal of Psychology* 142 (6): 615–631.

Ashoka (2010). What is a social entrepreneurship? Online at: www.ashoka.org/social_entrepreneur (accessed September 2012).

Balogun J, Wilmott H, Gleadle P, Hope-Hailey V (2005). Managing change across boundaries: boundary shaking practices. *British Journal of Management* 16: 261–278.

Bansal P (2003). From issues to action: the importance of individual concern and organisational values in responding to natural environmental issues. *Organisational Science* 14 (5): 510–527.

Barclay A (2010). Economic organisation culture. *Journal of Management Research* 2 (1): E6.

Barney JB (1991). Firm resources and sustained competitive advantage. *Journal of Management* 17 (1): 99–120.

Bendell J (2009). *The Corporate Responsibility Movement: Five Years of Global Corporate Responsibility Analysis from Lifeworth, 2001–2005.* Sheffield: Greenleaf.

BITC (2012). Shared goals, shared solutions: research on collaboration for a sustainable future. Online at: www.csreurope.org/data/files/npo/Collaboration_report_master.pdf.

BITC and Doughty Centre for Corporate Responsibility (2011). *The Business Case for Being a Responsible Business.* Cranfield: Cranfield University.

BITC and Doughty Centre for Corporate Responsibility (2013) *Towards a Sustainability Mindset: How Boards Organise Oversight and Governance of Corporate Responsibility.* London: BITC and The Doughty Centre for Corporate Responsibility.

Boston College Center for Corporate Citizenship – BCCCC (2010). *Profile of the Practice.* Online at: www.bcccc.net

Bower JL, Leonard HB, Painer LS (2011). Global capitalism at risk: what are you doing about it? September 2011, *Harvard Business Review.*

Buchanan D, Huczynski A (1997). *Organisational Behaviour: An Introductory Text.* London: Prentice Hall: UK.

Butcher D, Clarke M (2001). *Smart Management: Using Politics in Organisations.* Houndsmills: Palgrave.

Carson R (1962). *The Silent Spring.* Boston, MA: Houghton Mifflin: USA.

Chiaburu D, Lim A (2008). Manager trustworthiness or interactional justice? Predicting organisational citizenship behaviours. *Journal of Business Ethics* 83: 453–467.

Collier J, Esteban R (2007). Corporate social responsibility and employee commitment. *Business Ethics: A European Review* 16 (1): 19–33.

Cormack M (2012). *How to Guide: How to Identify a Company's Major Impacts – and Manage Them.* Cranfield, Bedford: Doughty Centre for Corporate Responsibility.

CPD Global 500 Climate Change report (2012). *Business Resilience in an Uncertain, Resource-Constrained World.* Online at: https://www.cdproject.net/en-us/Pages/global500.aspx (accessed November 2012).

Cramer J, Jonker J, van der Heijden A (2004). Making sense of corporate social responsibility. *Journal of Business Ethics* 55: 215–222.

CSR Asia (2008). *CSR in Asia: Who is Getting it Done?* Business report. Asia. Online at: http://www.csr-asia.com/report/report_csr_in_asia.pdf.

DARA (2012). Climate Vulnerability Monitor for further projections of the world in the near future. Online at: http://daraint.org/climate-vulnerability-monitor/climate-vulnerability-monitor-2012/.

Deal TE, Kennedy AA (1982). *Corporate Cultures.* Reading, MA: Addison-Wesley.

Drennan D (1992). *Transforming Company Culture.* London: McGraw-Hill.

Duarte F (2010). Working with corporate social responsibility in Brazilian Companies: the role of managers' values in the maintenance of CSR cultures. *Journal of Business Ethics* 96: 355–368.

Duarte F (2011). What does culture of corporate social responsibility look like? A glimpse into a Brazilian mining company. *International Journal of Business Anthropology* 2 (1): 106–122.

Eccles RG, Ioannou I, Serafeim G (2011). The impact of a corporate culture of sustainability on corporate behaviour and performance. *Harvard Business School Working Paper* 12-035.

Edelman (2012). *The Edelman Trust Barometer.* Online at: http://edelmaneditions.com/wp-content/uploads/2012/01/Final-Brochure-1.16.pdf (accessed November 2012).

Edmans A (2011). Does the stock market fully value intangibles? Employee satisfaction and equity prices. *Journal of Financial Economics* 101 (3): 621–640.

Elkington J (1997). *Cannibals with Forks.* London: Wiley.

Elkington J (2008a). *The Social Intrapreneur: A Field Guide for Change-Makers.* Online at: www.johnelkington.com/activities/reports.asp (accessed October 2012).

Elkington J (2008b). *The Power of Unreasonable People.* Harvard, MA: Harvard Business School Press.

Elkington J (2012). *The Zeronauts.* Abingdon, Oxon: Routledge.

Evans R, Davis W (2001). An examination of perceived corporate citizenship, job applicant attraction, and CSR work role definition. *Business and Society* 50: 465.

Exter N (2009). *How To: CR Champions Network.* Cranfield: Cranfield University.

Exter N (2011). *Engaging Employees in Corporate Responsibility.* Cranfield: Cranfield University. Online at: www.som.cranfield.ac.uk/som/dinamic-content/media/Engaging%20Employees%20in%20Corporate%20Responsibility.pdf.

Ferguson D (2010). *Measuring Business Value and Sustainability Performance.* Doughty Centre for Corporate Responsibility Occasional Paper. Online at: www.som.cranfield.ac.uk/som/dinamic-content/media/EABIS%20paper%20 final.doc.pdf.

Flank L (ed.) (2011). *Voices From the 99 Percent: An Oral History of the Occupy Wall Street Movement.* St Petersburg, FL: Red and Black Publishers.

Fortado L, Moshinsky B (2012). UBS rogue trader lawyers: risk didn't matter as long as you made money. *Business Insider.* Online at: www.businessinsider.com/kweku-adoboli-testimony-2012-9#ixzz2CfmZI5o5.

Frankl VE (1964). *Man's Search for Meaning: An Introduction to Logotherapy.* London: Hodder and Stoughton.

Freud S, Bonaparte M (eds) (2009). *The Origins of Psychoanalysis. Letters to Wilhelm Fliess: Drafts and Notes 1887–1902.* Whitefish, MT: Kessinger.

Frost P, Moore L, Reis Louis M, Lundberg C, Martin J (eds) (1991). *Reframing Organizational Culture.* Newbury Park, CA: Sage.

Fuchs C (2006). The self-organisation of social movements. *Systemic Practice and Action Research* 19 (1): 101–137.

GACSO (2011). *Defining and Developing the Corporate Sustainability Professional – The Practitioner's View.* Online at: www.gacso.org.

Gallup Engagement Index (2010) Online at: www.gallup.com/consulting.

George M (2002). *Lean Six Sigma: Combining Six Sigma with Lean Speed.* New York: McGraw Hill.

Gilman R (1990). Sustainability: The state of the movement. *In Context* 25 (55).

Gladwell M (2001). *The Tipping Point: How Little Things can Make a Big Difference.* London: Abacus.

Global Issues (2013). Poverty facts and statistics. www.globalissues.org/article/26/ poverty-facts-and-stats (accessed 7 January 2013).

Gond JP, El-Akremi A, Igalens J, Swaen V (2010). *CSR Influence on Employees.* Research Paper Series no. 54-2010. Nottingham: International Centre for Corporate Social Responsibility, Nottingham University Business School.

Graafland J, van de Ven B (2006). Strategic and moral motivation for corporate social responsibility. *Journal of Corporate Citizenship* 22: 111–123.

Graen GB, Scandura TA (1987). Toward a psychology of dyadic organizing, in Cummings LL and Staw B (Eds) *Research in Organizational Behavior*, vol. 9 (pp. 175–208). Greenwich, CT: JAI.

Grayson D (2008). The CR management black-hole. *Management Focus* Autumn, 6–9.

Grayson D, Nelson J (2013). *Corporate Responsibility Coalitions: The Past, Present and Future of Alliances for Sustainable Capitalism.* Sheffield: Greenleaf.

Grayson D, McLaren M, Spitzeck H (2011). Social Intrapreneurs – an extra force for sustainability. Cranfield: Cranfield University.

Grayson D, Spitzeck H, Alt E, McLaren M (2013). *Social Intrapreneurs.* Sheffield: Greenleaf.

Handy C (1993). *Understanding Organisations*, 4th edn. London: Penguin Books.

Hawken P (2008). *Blessed Unrest.* New York: Penguin Books.

Hayes J (2007). *The Theory and Practice of Change Management.* Basingstoke: Palgrave Macmillan, p. 95.

Hemingway CA, Maclagan PW (2004). Managers' personal values as drivers of corporate social responsibility. *Journal of Business Ethics* 50: 33–44.

Hofstede G (1984). *Culture's Consequences: International Differences in Work-Related Values*, 2nd edn. Beverly Hills, CA: Sage.

Houchin K, Maclean D (2005). Complexity theory and strategic change: an empirically informed critique. *British Journal of Management* 16: 149–166.

Inman P (2009). Financial Services Authority Chairman backs tax on 'socially useless' banks. *Guardian* 27 August.

International Labour Office (2012). *Global Employment Trends 2012*. Online at: www.ilo.org/wcmsp5/groups/public/@dgreports/@dcomm/@publ/documents/publication/wcms_171571.pdf (accessed October 2012).

Johnson G, Scholes K (2005). *Exploring Corporate Strategy*, 6th edn. London: Prentice Hall.

Kaye L (2012). Time to start valuing human capital as an asset on the balance sheet. *Guardian Sustainable Business online*: Thursday 2 August 2012 (accessed August 2012).

Kobayashi E, Kerbo HR, Sharp SF (2010). Differences in individual and collective tendencies among college students in Japan and US. *International Journal of Comparative Sociology* 51 (1–2): 59–84.

Kotter J (1995). Leading change: why transformation efforts fail. *Harvard Business Review* January 2007; original article 1995.

Kram KE, Hall DT (1995). Mentoring in a context of diversity and turbulence, in Lobel S, and Kossek E (Eds), *Human Resource Strategies for Managing Diversity*. London: Blackwell.

Lawrence TB, Dyck B, Maitlis S, Mauws MK (2006). The underlying structure of continuous change. *MITSloan Management Review* 47 (4): 59–66.

Leopold A (1949). *A Sand County Almanac*. New York: Oxford University Press.

Lesser EL, Storck J (2001). Communities of practice and organisational performance. *Knowledge Management* 40 (4): 831–841.

Liebowitz J (2010). The role of HR in achieving a sustainability culture. *Journal of Sustainable Development* 3 (4): 50–57.

Lim B (1995). Examining the organizational culture and organizational performance link. *Journal of Leadership and Organization Development Journal* 16 (5): 16–21.

Lovelock J (1979). *Gaia: A New Look at Life on Earth*. Oxford: Oxford University Press.

Lyon D (2004). How can you help organisations change to meet the corporate responsibility agenda? *Corporate Social Responsibility and Environmental Management* 11 (3): 133–139.

Makhlouf H (2011). Social entrepreneurship: generating solutions to global challenges. *International Journal of Management and Information Systems* 15 (1): 1–8.

Marks & Spencer (2012). *The Key Lessons from the Plan A Business Case*. London: Marks & Spencer.

Martin R, Osberg S (2007). Social entrepreneurship: the case for definition. *Stanford Social Innovation Review* Spring: 28–39.

McGuire SJJ (2003). *Entrepreneurial Organizational Culture: Construct Definition and Instrument Development and Validation*. Ph.D. dissertation. Washington, DC: George Washington University.

McLaren M (2010). *Supporting Corporate Responsibility Performance Through Effective Knowledge Management*. Cranfield: Doughty Centre for Corporate Responsibility.

Meadows D, Meadows D, Randers J (1972). *The Limits to Growth.* New York: Universe Books. [Updated in 1993 and 2004.]

Meyerson D (2001). *Tempered Radicals. How People use Difference to Inspire Change at Work.* Boston, MA: Harvard Business Press.

Mirvis P, Googins B, with Kiser (2012). Corporate social innovation. Paper in progress as of November 2012.

Mirvis P (2012). Employee engagement and CSR: transactional, relational and developmental approaches. *California Management Review* 54 (4): 93–117.

MIT Global Climate Solutions Model (2012). Online at: http://globalchange.mit.edu/files/document/Outlook2012.pdf.

Neate R (2012). Tearful trader Kweku Adoboli tells trial 'UBS was my family'. *The Guardian* Friday 26 October 2012. Online at: www.guardian.co.uk/business/2012/oct/26/trader-kweku-adoboli-trial-ubs

Net Impact (2012). *Talent Report: What Workers Want in 2012.* Online at: www.netimpact.org/learning-resources/research/what-workers-want (accessed September 2012).

Orlitzky O, Schmidt FL, Tynes SL (2003). Corporate social and financial performance: a meta-analysis. *Organisational Studies* 24 (3): 403–441.

OSI (2008). Office of Science and Innovation definition, UK, from DSTL, Department of Defence. UK presentation.

Parker S, Bindl U, Strauss K (2010). Making things happen: a model of proactive motivation. *Journal of Management* 36 (4): 827–856.

Pedersen ER (2010). Modelling CSR: how managers understand the responsibilities of business towards society. *Journal of Business Ethics* 91: 155–166.

Pichardo N (1997). New social movements: a critical review. *Annual Review of Sociology* 23: 411–430.

Porter M (1990). *The Competitive Advantage of Nations.* London: Palgrave.

Porter M, Kramer M (2011). Creating shared value. *Harvard Business Review* 89 (1/2): 62–77.

Posner BZ, Schmidt WH (1993). Values congruence and differences between the interplay of personal and organizational value systems. *Journal of Business Ethics* 12 (5): 341–347.

PWC (2011). *CEO Survey: Growth Reimagined.* Online at: www.pwc.com/gx/en/ceo-survey/pdfs/paul_polman.pdf.

PWC (2012). *Sustainability Valuation: An Oxymoron?* Online at: www.pwc.com/en_US/us/transaction-services/publications/assets/pwc-sustainability-valuation.pdf.

Ragins B, Scandura T (1999). Burden or blessing? Expected costs and benefits of being a mentor. *Journal of Organisational Behaviour* 20: 493–509.

Ralston E (2009). Deviance or norm? Exploring corporate social responsibility. *European Business Review* 22 (4): 397–410.

Ravasi D, Schultz M (2006). Responding to organizational identity threats: exploring the role of organizational culture. *Academy of Management Journal* 49 (3): 433–458.

Reker GT, Wong PTP (1988). Aging as an individual process: Toward a theory of personal meaning. In JE Birren and VL Bengston (Eds.) *Emergent Theories of Aging* (pp. 214–246). New York, NY: Springer.

Reker GT, Peacock EJ, Wong PT (1987). Meaning and purpose in life and well-being: A life span perspective. *Journal of Gerontology* 42: 44–49.

Rockström J, Steffen W, Noone K, Persson A, Chapin FS, Lambin E, Lenton TM *et al.* (2009). Planetary boundaries: exploring the safe operating space for humanity. *Ecology and Society* 14 (2): 32.

Sabeti H (2011). To reform capitalism, CEOs should champion structural reforms. *Harvard Business Review* October 18.

Scandura TA, Tejeda MJ, Werther WB, Lankau MJ (1996). Perspectives on mentoring. *Leadership and Organization Development Journal* 17 (3): 50–56.

Schein E (2006). *Career Anchors*. San Francisco: Wiley.

Schein E (2010). *Organisational Culture and Leadership*. San Francisco: Jossey-Bass.

Second Half (2010). The Second Half: Ageing, Entrepreneurship and Sustainability. Online at: www.som.cranfield.ac.uk/som/p16340/Research/Research-Centres/Doughty-Centre-Home/Knowledge-Creation/Library-of-work/Document-Library (accessed December 2012).

Senge P (2008). *The Necessary Revolution*. London: Nicholas Brealey Publishing.

Sharma D, Borna S, Stearns J (2009). An investigation of the effect of corporate ethical values on employee commitment and performance: examining the moderating role of perceived fairness. *Journal of Business Ethics* 89: 251–260.

Sirota D, Mischkind LA, Meltzer MI (2005). *The Enthusiastic Employee*. Upper Saddle River, NJ: Wharton School Publishing.

Sirota Survey Intelligence (2007). Workers satisfied with company's social responsibility are more engaged and positive. Online at: www.sirota.com/pdfs/Workers_Satisfied_With_Companys_Social_Responsibility_Are_More_Positive_and_Engaged.pdf

Snow D, Soule SA, Kriesi H (2004). *The Blackwell Companion to Social Movements*. Oxford: Wiley-Blackwell.

Song MK (2009). The integrative structure of employee commitment. *Leadership and Organisational Development* 30 (3): 240–255.

Song JH, Kim HM (2008). The integrative structure of employee commitment. *Leadership and Organization Development Journal* 30 (3): 240–255.

Sosik J, Lee D (2002). Mentoring in organisations: A social judgement perspective for developing tomorrow's leaders. *Journal of Leadership Studies* 8 (4): 17–32.

Stern N (2008). The Stern review: economics of climate change. Online at: http://www.hm-treasury.gov.uk/d/Executive_Summary.pdf (accessed November 2012).

Stern N (2009). *A Blueprint for a Safer Planet*. London: Bodley Head

Swanson DL (1995). Addressing a theoretical problem by reorienting the corporate social performance model. *Academy of Management Review* 20 (1): 43–64.

Swap W, Leonard D, Shields M, Abrams L (2001). Using mentoring and storytelling to transfer knowledge in the workplace. *Journal of Management Information Systems* 18 (1): 95–114.

Thaler R (2008). *Nudge: Choice Architecture can Nudge People Towards Better Decisions and Experiences*. New Haven, CT: Yale University Press.

Touraine A (1985). An introduction to the study of social movements. *Social Research* 52 (4): 749–787.

Turker D (2009). How corporate social responsibility influences organisational commitment. *Journal of Business Ethics* 89: 189–204.

United Nations (1987). *Report of the World Commission on Environment and Development*. Brundtland Report. General Assembly Resolution 42/187, 11 December 1987.

Valentino CL, Francis WH (2004). The role of middle managers in the transmission and integration of organisational culture. *Journal of Healthcare Management* 49 (6): 393–404.

Visser W (2008). *Making a Difference: Purpose-Inspired Leadership for Corporate Sustainability and Responsibility.* Staarbrucken: VDM.

Waddock S (2008). *The Difference Makers.* Sheffield: Greenleaf.

Washington M, Hacker M (2005). Why change fails: knowledge counts. *Leadership and Organization Development Journal* 26 (5/6): 400–411.

Weber Y (1996). Corporate cultural fit and performance in mergers and acquisitions. *Human Relations* 49 (9): 1181–1202.

Weintrobe S (2013). *Engaging with Climate Change: Psychoanalytic and Interdisciplinary Perspectives.* Abingdon, Oxon: Routledge.

Wenger E, McDermott R, Snyder WM (2002). *Cultivating Communities of Practice.* Cambridge, MA: Harvard Business School Press.

Whitehouse L (2006). Corporate social responsibility: views from the frontline. *Journal of Business Ethics* 63: 279–296.

Willcoxson L, Millet B (2000). The management of organisational culture. *Australian Journal of Management and Organisational Behaviour* 3 (2): 91–99.

Williamson I, Burnett M, Bartol K (2009). The interactive effect of collectivism and organisational rewards on affective organisational commitment. *Cross Cultural Management: An International Journal* 16 (1): 28–43.

World Commission on Environment and Development (1987). *Our Common Future.* New York: Oxford University Press.

Zald M (2005). The strange career of an idea and its resurrection: social movements in organizations. *Journal of Management Inquiry* 14 (2): 157–166.

Index